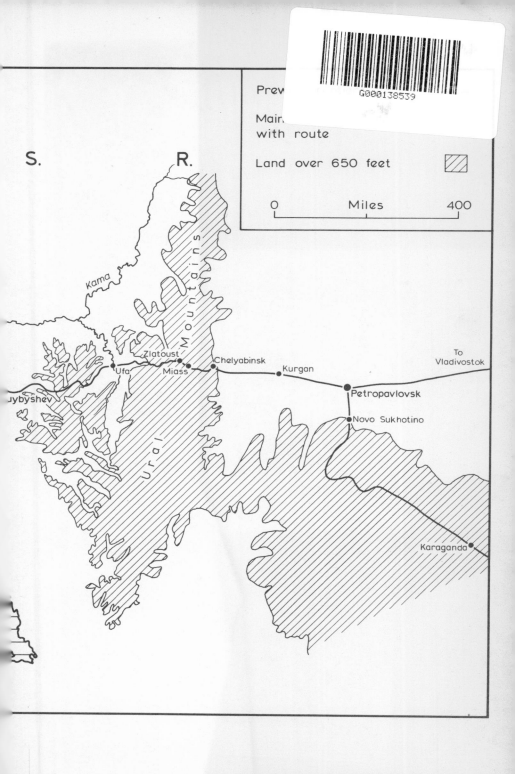

S.   R.

Prev

Main
with route

Land over 650 feet

0   Miles   400

Kama

Mountains

Zlatoust

Ufa   Miass   Chelyabinsk

Kurgan

Petropavlovsk

To
Vladivostok

Novo Sukhotino

U r a l

uybyshev

Karaganda

The Silver Madonna

*Eugenia Wasilewska today (seated) with
her daughter Marguerite and grandchildren*

The Silver Madonna

OR

THE ODYSSEY OF
EUGENIA WASILEWSKA

London
GEORGE ALLEN & UNWIN LTD
RUSKIN HOUSE MUSEUM STREET

FIRST PUBLISHED IN 1970

© *George Allen and Unwin Ltd, 1970*

ISBN 0 04 920029 1

PRINTED IN GREAT BRITAIN
in 11 point Baskerville type
BY COX AND WYMAN LTD
FAKENHAM

Foreword

BY ARTHUR COOK

The story of Eugenia Wasilewska might never have been told if she had not made her way to London in 1953 with her daughter, then a sturdy child of twelve. The years before had seen her flight from the Russian army, through what is now East Germany and into West Germany, and the incredible hardships of a mother alone, trying to exist and bring up a daughter in the post-war days of a defeated nation.

London was not the end of the struggle but it was there that I met Eugenia. She was working as a seamstress and Marguerite, whose languages were Polish and German, was now at an English school. Eugenia told me sometimes of her childhood and what had been her family's estates, now destroyed by the Russians; she spoke of her brother whom she did not know to be alive or dead and to my question, 'Where did you last see him?', came the simple and quiet reply, 'In Siberia, I escaped from there.'

Gradually Eugenia's story unfolded, the events, the incidents, the tragedies of the years before she remembered as though they were yesterday. The names, the places, dates and people, they were indelibly engraved on her mind, never to be removed. She remembered them all and when I inquired if the escape had been before or after Marguerite was born came the reply, 'I was carrying her, I was pregnant. That is why I escaped from Siberia.'

She showed me the faded photographs of her happy childhood days, her father, her brother and what had once been the family mansion. She showed me the small silver plaque of the Madonna which had been with her always, the symbol of the courage, determination and endurance which had safely brought herself and Marguerite through all the years of hardship.

'You must write of those years,' I told Eugenia and she replied, "One day – when Marguerite is old enough to understand.'

In March 1969 a letter from Canada reached me in Libya, it was from Eugenia and it read. . . .

'I am at last happily married and I have two lovely grandchildren. Through my many hardships I have gained new experience, with the help of the silver Madonna and Her blessing. Now I would like my story printed as a book as a memory for Marguerite and her children – so that they will appreciate and never forget the freedom in which they live.'

Contents

CHAPTER I

Russian Occupation

Christmas Day, 1939, and the snow lay thick in the small town of Aleksandriya, near the Russian border in eastern Poland. Not that the border meant anything to us any more. For three months our land had been occupied by the Russians and many times I had wondered if it might not have been better, after all, if the Germans had conquered the whole of Poland.

The tiny room I shared with my brother Jurek was freezing; for hours I had struggled to make a fire from the damp wood and now we were sitting at our Christmas meal. We sat wearing every piece of clothing we could wrap around our shivering bodies. At least the soup was hot, and for days I had saved the vegetables for this special feast of soup and rye bread.

We spoke hardly a word. There seemed nothing left to talk about. I had cried all the way home from midnight mass the night before and there were no tears left. I helped Jurek to more soup and he gave me a tired smile of thanks. The meal, the best we had had in weeks, was over and we pushed the dishes aside. Jurek wearily picked up a book and began to study the lesson he had to give at the local school next day. Everything was quiet, the quietness that only thick snow can bring.

It was barely four months since that day, September 1st, when the radio suddenly went dead and I heard the terrifying screams of the German dive-bombers. Life had been happy for me until then, with the serene, childish happiness of a gentle convent education. I was seventeen and should have returned from my holiday to the convent near Warsaw if those bombs had not dropped, if Germany had not attacked us, suddenly and viciously as she did.

Just sixteen days later Germany and Russia partitioned

Poland; the Bolsheviks were coming again, but I cannot
remember any feeling of dread until the day when they took
father away and put him in prison.

His crime? Father was a wealthy landowner. Two thousand
acres of beautiful farmland and woodland swept over the gentle
hills around the big house. He was loved by every tenant farmer
and villager for miles around. But he was an 'enemy' of the
Communist way of life. Some time, we were told, he would be
tried by a people's court for his so-called crime. Mother was
half Polish and half Russian and had died when I was a tiny
child. Henryk Laessig, my father, part Hungarian and part
German, had married again and I had a small stepbrother,
Henryk.

The Russian soldiers had looted the house and we were turned
out. For a while we had lived in a small house on the estate, but
the Russians would not leave us alone. If we dug potatoes they
would take them 'for the army', and as the food got shorter
Jurek, now nineteen, left for Aleksandriya and a job as a
teacher, and I followed soon afterwards.

Poor Jurek! He was working so hard: classes in the morning
and afternoon for children, and more classes at night for old and
illiterate people. He did his best to look after me. With father in
prison, the two of us were almost alone in the world, and night
after night I would sit, wrapped in a blanket, helping him to
correct the children's lesson papers.

Every day we heard more stories of how the people around
us were being taken to Siberia as slave labour. They were going
in hundreds, thousands, and one day I had heard that among
the latest batch was one of my father's foresters, Kuczynski.

I discovered that he was being held in the Jewish synagogue in
Aleksandriya and I hurried there, trying to see him. I failed, but
I saw for the first time the treatment I was to expect from the
Russians. Kuczynski's wife was there, weeping and pleading to
the guards to be allowed to see her husband as she clutched her
baby to her and her little boy clung to her skirts. With the
hundreds of other women and children she was pushed away
with rifles and bayonets.

Two weeks later Kuczynski's wife and children were arrested;
all I heard was that she was taken away on a train with hundreds

of others. I never saw or heard of the family again. Our turn must come, we knew.

We went to our beds early that Christmas night, it was warmer there and sleep could wipe away the dread of the morrow. It was usually like that: a prayer of thanks that we had been spared another day and a prayer that the knock would not come on the door early the following morning.

In February came news of the biggest mass arrest so far. On the Polish–Russian border were hundreds of farmers and their families, Polish soldiers and officers who had been given the land after the First World War in an attempt to make the border strong. At three o'clock one morning the Russians swooped; every farmer and his family, thousands in all, was arrested and taken away. The Russians looked on them as one of the biggest dangers in any possible uprising.

Many of the farmers lay on the floor and refused to go, we were told, but the Russians took the wives and children and the men were forced to follow. Others escaped but had to return to the prisoners' marshalling points if they ever wanted to see their families again. In one day the border was cleared, but where the farmers went nobody knew. Some rumours said that they were bound for Siberia, others said that they had been sent north to the forests near Moscow.

It was in that same month, February, that Jurek and I had the chance to get away from the Ukraine and from the Russians. In the province of Wolyn lived several thousand Germans, and under the Soviet–German Agreement on the partition of Poland the Russians had agreed with Germany that any of these Germans who wished could return to Germany with all their possessions. Many were moving just now.

Jurek knew lots of them, and one day three Ukrainian Germans came to see us. 'Come with us,' they tried to persuade Jurek. 'This may be your only chance to escape and you can come with us as a German.' To me it seemed the only possible way out, but Jurek was adamant. 'I know my name is German,' he said, 'but I am not a German. Why should I go with you to die in the Maginot Line? I would rather be sent to Siberia and die there, a Pole.'

That night we saw an old aunt. She had been born of Austrian parents who came to the Ukraine in 1918 and she was going to Germany under the scheme. She, too, tried to persuade Jurek to go; she said that perhaps he could arrange father's release from there, but Jurek would not hear of it. 'Why should I go to fight for something I do not believe in?' he asked, and the subject was never mentioned again. The Germans and our aunt left, and we stayed with the Russians.

In March came the elections under the new Communist constitution. Three men were candidates for the Aleksandriya area, but the only difference between them was in name. They were all Communists.

Polling was to take place in the school hall, the largest in the town. I was eighteen that year, the age when in Russia a girl can vote, and Jurek thought that he should take me to the poll.

We met many Russians. Few of them were in uniform and they seemed friendly and homely. They appeared to like Jurek and were surprised to know that he had a sister. One officer asked me what I did, and when I told him that I was looking after Jurek, he laughed. 'He is a big fellow and should look after himself,' he said. 'A fine girl like you should work for herself. All women do in Russia. They are the same as men.'

Everyone was so pleasant to me. Drinks were passed around and a balalaika band was playing as the people came and went from the poll. I do not know who suggested it, but Jurek suddenly came to me and said, 'We must dance – together.'

We did dance, the oberek, a graceful Polish dance, and it was a huge success. The Russians applauded loudly. They asked if I had been trained at a ballet school, said I must visit them again and must go to their evening political classes. I promised I would and Jurek and I left at three o'clock that afternoon amid loud 'goodbyes'. I felt all was well; I am sure Jurek thought so too, until the next day.

Jurek came home from school early in the afternoon. I sensed something was wrong, as he had never before been home until the evening. His face was white; he sank into a chair and buried his face in his hands. It was minutes before he spoke. 'Today I was ordered to write my life story,' he said slowly. 'Everything had to be put down in ink, when and where I was born, where

I went to school and who and what my father was.' Jurek paused. 'I told the truth,' he said.

My heart was pounding as Jurek finished the story, 'The head teacher sent for me and told me that he had no idea I was the son of a landowner. He told me that because of this I should never have had the job. He ordered me from the school. Told me never to return. He said these were orders from his superiors.'

Before Jurek left, the head teacher had given him advice. He had liked my brother, had liked his work. 'Take your sister and go to a town where you are not known,' he had told Jurek. 'Change your name and get another job.' Jurek wrung his hands as he looked up at me. 'What is the use?' he asked. 'Wherever we go I shall be asked the same questions. If I lie and am found out we shall both be punished.'

Neither of us talked much for the rest of that day. We knew that the time was short before we would be sent away like the rest. To stay at the house where we were living was impossible. For three days we searched for somewhere to live, but always we were told the same. Even people who had been great friends turned us away. It was as though we had a disease. Everyone knew that our turn to be taken away was coming soon; everyone was scared to take us, to be seen talking to us. When we went back to our room the Russians said it was needed for another teacher.

At last, nearly dropping with exhaustion from tramping the snowbound streets, we were taken in by the wife of a priest. She had a son and a daughter about the same age as Jurek and me, and when we thanked her for her kindness she said, 'It can make no difference if you live with us. We are in the same position as yourselves, suffering from the same illness. We may be taken away any day.'

Everywhere in Aleksandriya, Polish officials were being replaced by Communists; we could hardly go anywhere without the fear of a Communist pointing his finger at us. Jurek wore Russian-type clothes, but I was conspicuous as I had only my winter school clothes, the navy blue skirt, blue blouse and blue coat with silver buttons, and the badge on the sleeve giving the number of my school

Jurek had little money left now, but one day he gave me some.

'Go to Rovno,' he said. 'Buy some clothes, peasant clothes, anything which will make you look like the other people here.'

Early the next morning I went to Aleksandriya station for the train to Rovno, but every carriage was crammed full and the platform was crowded with others who could not get into the train and faced a freezing wait until the next day. I despaired of ever reaching Rovno, but at the last minute luck came to me. Just as the train was about to move I heard shouts from a nearby carriage. Three boys from our own village, Zaborol, had recognized me; they pulled me through the carriage window and somehow pushed me into a corner.

At Rovno I went to a dentist friend of my father. Round my neck in a small leather bag I carried what was left of my mother's jewellery and to the dentist I sold my mother's wedding ring and a bracelet. The dentist wanted the gold for teeth – the Russians were proud of gold teeth – and I got enough money to buy some clothes.

I stayed the night with the dentist and his family and at three in the morning I was in a long queue outside a large Rovno store. No one knew if there would be anything for sale that day, but for hours we stood in the snow and cold. Some of the people had lit small fires in the gutters in an attempt to keep warm, but I shivered endlessly. Thousands of us were waiting and at every few yards was a Russian soldier with a fixed bayonet.

I never reached the main door of the store, for at nine in the morning a large notice was put up: there was nothing to sell that day. The Russian soldiers closed in; they feared that the crowd would storm the store in desperation. The next night I was at the store at midnight. Again thousands of people queued in the frozen streets. And again at nine o'clock next morning we were told that there was nothing to sell that day.

I was choking back tears as I made my way back once more, I was so cold that I thought I was ill. Then the dentist's wife searched through her clothes and found me a three-quarter length coat. It was lined with fur – dog's fur, I thought – brown with white spots, by no means new; but the dentist's wife pressed it on me and would not accept money. It would hide my school uniform. She said I must take it.

The following day I felt much better and set out for the

station early. I had plenty of time to catch the train, I thought, but I had not gone far when I saw a huge procession marching down the main street towards me. Thousands of young men were carrying banners. 'Long live Stalin, long live freedom, long live the workers', they proclaimed. I was forced off the main road and had to take side roads. Whenever I tried to get back to the main road I met the processions. It took over an hour for what should have been a fifteen-minute journey until at last I reached the station. The train had gone.

I did not know what to do. I felt lost. Then a woman spoke to me. She told me there would be no other train that day. 'There is only one way to get there,' she said. 'We must walk.'

On to the railway line we clambered and began the long walk to Aleksandriya. It was not difficult over the hard snow along the line and we walked for over an hour. On either side of us now there was open country, and parked on a siding in front of us was a long line of railway wagons.

We were halfway along the line of wagons when a man suddenly jumped on to the line in front of us. He was in soldier's uniform and carried a gun with fixed bayonet. His face was ugly, like a Mongolian; his eyes squinted and he leered at me as we stopped. 'Where are you going?' he demanded, and the woman told him that we were walking to Aleksandriya. 'Where are your papers?' he asked as he leered at me again. My heart sank; I had no papers. Quickly the woman produced hers. She worked for a Russian commissar and her papers gave her permission to travel. I told the soldier that I had no papers and his face twisted into a grin. He waved his bayonet at the woman: 'You go,' he ordered, 'but the young one must stay here with me.'

I was terrified. The soldier was laughing now. 'You go,' he ordered again, but the woman refused. 'If she stays, I stay too; she is my friend,' she told him and at this the soldier became annoyed. 'Go!' he shouted this time. 'You silly old woman, I don't want you, I want the young one.'

Again he ordered her to go and again the woman refused. The bayonet was near her stomach as suddenly she shouted 'Run!' and we ran as fast as we could down the line. We were scared that the soldier would shoot, but no shot came. He shouted

B

'Stop, stop!' but his shouts became fainter as we ran. We did not slow down for a long time.

At seven o'clock that night, after nearly four hours of walking, we reached Aleksandriya and I said goodbye to my woman friend. I hurried home to Jurek, told him what had happened and his face looked worried. 'Never again must you go to Rovno,' he said. 'You must not even be seen too much around Aleksandriya. You must go only to our own village.'

It was not long before we were without food again and I decided to go to Zaborol to see the head man of the village. He gave me bread, flour and a few vegetables; he asked me if I would like a cow, but I laughed. 'What would I do with a cow?' I asked. 'I could not keep it.'

Where we lived the priest's wife kept two cows and there was just enough food and grazing for them. She gave us a little milk when we needed it, but now I had an idea. 'I would like a little pig,' I told the head man, and it was his turn to laugh. 'Whatever would you do with a pig?' he asked, and I told him that I would bring it up and kill it when it was big enough to eat.

The villagers brought me a baby pig and some barley to feed it with. But in a week our food was gone and we did not want to beg in the village for more. Now we could only wait for the kindly villagers of Zaborol, who sometimes made the journey to Aleksandriya with food for us – their children, as they felt.

From them we heard news of our stepmother. She was still at the house, but planning, we were told, to go to Rovno. She hoped to disappear there under another name and no longer visited the prison where my father was, because she was not allowed near.

Things were becoming desperate for Jurek and me. It was almost impossible to get food. Then came the second chance for us to lead a normal life.

Whilst he was teaching Jurek had as pupil the daughter of a Russian commissar; she was sixteen, reasonably pretty and in her girlish way was very fond of Jurek. She told her father that she wanted to marry Jurek and so insisted that one day the father sent Jurek a message. 'If you marry the girl,' he said, 'the commissar promises that you will get your job back. He also promises that no harm will come to your sister and no charges will ever be brought against either of you.'

Jurek did not wait a moment before he replied. 'Thank you,' he told the messenger. 'I like the girl, I think she is charming, but I would not marry her just for my security. She wants to marry me because I am different, because I am the son of a landowner. Tell the commissar I say no.'

The messenger pointed out that if he married, Jurek would become a citizen of the Soviet Union. He said that I would be able to go to school again, but still Jurek refused to marry the girl. His principles would not allow him to take this easy road to freedom.

The commissar was polite. He sent back a message that he could not make Jurek marry his daughter if he did not wish to. But he was sorry. Jurek and I wondered what would happen now, and we did not go out for days.

It was then that we were almost pleased that father was in jail. He was still at Rovno, we knew; it seemed that he was safer in prison than outside. It had been weeks since we had heard any news of him when one night a man knocked at our door. He had just been released from Rovno jail, where he and my father had shared the same cell. In it, with them, were thieves, murderers, a blacksmith, and a policeman. Father had been elected as senior of the cell, because he was so kind and helpful to the rest; he was still reasonably fit and when our visitor had last seen him, father was mending his clothes with a needle made from a bone and thread unpicked from his socks.

Father had sent us an urgent message. 'He asked me to tell you to go to German-occupied Poland at once,' said the man. 'He does not know when he will be released from jail, if ever, and says that it is better for you to be among civilized people than stay here among the Russians.'

Again Jurek refused; he did not want to be conscripted into the German army and said that I could go alone. In the months to come I often wished I had done so, but at the same time the thought terrified me. I was but a schoolgirl, and Jurek was the only person I could cling to now.

Two weeks later, on April 13th, the blow fell. It was eight o'clock in the morning; I was dressed, but Jurek was walking

around our one room in his bare feet and looking for a pair of
socks. A Russian commissar walked into the room. 'You are
Jurek Laessig?' he asked and Jurek nodded. 'Your mother is
outside in a wagon,' said the commissar. 'She wishes you to
join her.'

Jurek continued to look for his socks. 'She is not my mother,'
he told the commissar. 'If she wants to go anywhere she can go
alone.' Jurek was not interested, but the commissar spoke again.
'You must come,' said the commissar; 'your father is waiting at
the goods station at Lubomirka. He is going to Russia to start a
new life and he wishes to take his family with him.'

In a moment Jurek was almost beside himself with excitement. 'Hurry, Eugenia!' he almost shouted at me. 'If papa is at
the station we must go quickly. It does not matter where they
send us so long as we are with papa.'

The commissar told us to take everything we could carry,
clothes, food, even a mattress, but Jurek was too excited to
bother about any of this. He was almost dancing around the
room. 'Who wants to take anything?' he said. 'Nothing matters
so long as we are with papa again.' He would not pack a thing.
I had to do it all.

I packed quickly; into a little canvas bag which I hung
around my neck I put everything of value we possessed. There
were about three hundred roubles in money, still left from the
sale to the dentist, my mother's engagement ring, a gold chain
with a locket set in diamonds and a tiny picture of mother in it.
There was father's gold watch-chain, his own gold watch and
mother's, two gold bracelets and some ear-rings. In a case I
quickly packed the thing I treasured most: a silver head of the
Madonna, about two and a half inches by two inches and set in
a gold filigree miniature altar, which opened and closed like a
book.

Outside the house a small crowd had gathered to see what was
going on. The priest's wife had thought that the Russians had
come for her and she had sent for her husband. The priest
quickly finished a sermon he was delivering at the church and
ran down the street towards the house. Outside stood a large
wagon and on it sat my stepmother. She was dressed in a thick
fur coat, and her small son Henryk was leaning on her, asleep.

But they were not alone. I was surprised when I recognized the others: my stepmother's parents, an aunt, a brother and his wife and their baby, Barbara, a few months old.

My stepmother looked at us but said nothing as we threw our belongings on to the wagon and the horses moved off towards Lubomirka. It had been three o'clock that morning when the Russians had gone to the farm where my stepmother lived with her parents. They had asked where Jurek and I were, and my stepmother had told them simply 'Aleksandriya', but they had collected us as they had passed through on the way to Lubomirka. The aunt, brother and his wife had been found in Rovno the previous day; they had been living under assumed names, but this did not help them when the time came.

We were the last to arrive at the goods station at Lubomirka and there I saw the sight which I had tried to imagine as I lay in bed at night, wondering about the day which had to come. On a siding stood the cattle trucks, covered and with large doors on the sides which slid open. In each truck were crammed women, young men and children, sitting on top of the bundles, mattresses and cases they had been ordered to bring.

I recognized the family of a shopkeeper from Zaborol. I saw a woman who had once been our servant in the big house and was now the wife of a policeman. I saw children crying and tiny babies lying on top of the piles of baggage. Everywhere they seemed to be asking the same question, 'Where is my husband?' or 'Where is my father?' We searched the scene with our eyes, but could see no men waiting there, no man who could have been father.

The Russians had told everyone the same story. They had promised everyone that father or husband would be waiting at the station and now everyone seemed to be shouting the same question at once.

Jurek and I jumped from our wagon and ran to a commissar who, by his gaudy uniform, appeared to be in charge. We asked him the question which was on everyone's lips and his face broke into a slight grin. 'I am sorry but you were late arriving,' he said. 'We could not wait and had to send the men on ahead in another train. You must pack your luggage into a truck now and you will catch up with your father later.'

Jurek and I looked at each other. Could we believe what the commissar had told us? I know that deep down in our hearts we both were realizing already that this had been merely a trick to get us to the station with as little fuss as possible.

By eleven o'clock the doors were closed all along the train. I could not tell how many were in the truck; there was so much baggage that we could hardly move. I climbed on to the mattress which was at the top of the pile and just sat, hour after hour. From the voices inside the truck it seemed that there were dozens of people; some were weeping, others were asking each other the eternal question. 'Where are we going?'

CHAPTER II

Slow Train to Siberia

It was afternoon and the train had not moved. Jurek and I had had nothing to eat that day. Other people in the truck had brought food, but no one knew for how long they would have to make it last. Jurek and I could not beg food from them. My stomach was aching with hunger and I wondered how long I could last out.

At three o'clock we heard voices outside the truck and the door slid open with a bang. There stood the priest's wife and she was carrying a huge enamel bowl. She pointed when she saw Jurek and me. 'There they are,' she cried to the commissar. 'They left without taking their food this morning. I have brought it for them.'

When we had been taken away she had killed one of the pigs, not our own small pig but hers. She had killed four chickens and had cooked them, had quickly made two large, round and flat rye loaves and had filled a bag with salt. Then she had hurried to the goods station, hoping that we would still be there.

The food was handed up to us and the door slammed shut. We hardly had time to thank the priest's wife, but I saw her sweet, kind face trying to smile through the tears.

Now we had plenty of food and Jurek and I had the best meal for days. But as the day wore on there came another worry. There was no milk for the tiny baby Barbara; her mother could not feed her from the breast and the baby began to cry.

She was still crying in the early hours of the next morning when there was a sudden jolt. Many of us were thrown off the mattresses and baggage. We were moving, we were starting the journey, nobody knew whither.

Hours later the train shuddered to a stop, the doors were pulled open and a guard shouted to us to take buckets and get water. Jurek and I grabbed buckets and jumped to the ground. We were somewhere in Polesie, we knew. On one side of us was open, barren country and on the other a wood. The guard pointed towards the wood and shouted: 'There is a ditch, get your water.'

We hurried into the wood with the others and found the ditch. We were bending over it when I realized that the guard was not with us and I turned to Jurek. 'Let us escape now,' I whispered. 'The people of Polesie hate the Bolsheviks and will help us to get to Germany. It may be our only chance and we have not yet gone far.'

I was surprised at Jurek's answer; I no longer expected him to be stubborn about going to Germany. Now, I thought he would realize that anything would be preferable to going back to the cattle train. But he refused. 'Why should I go to Germany?' he asked. 'I don't like Germany. I want to see papa.'

Jurek must have known that I did not believe we would see father at the end of this journey, for he quickly added: 'And if we don't see papa, we are at least seeing some of the world for nothing. We are not even paying for a train ticket.'

I tried to argue, but Jurek quickly stopped me. 'We are young,' he said, 'we are strong and healthy. Perhaps some of the old ones will die, but we shall not. It would be silly to run away now. We shall come out of this.'

With the buckets full of water from the rapidly melting snow we walked back to the train, the doors were slammed shut and the train moved off. I climbed back on top of the baggage and sat quietly thinking. I was almost wishing that I had tried to escape alone, but I knew Jurek would never have allowed that.

On went the train until the evening and we covered roughly two hundred miles in a north-easterly direction before we pulled into Sarny. Here the European railway gauge ended and the wider Russian gauge began. On a siding we were ordered from one truck into another. We were all trying to hold on to our possessions and when we were finally aboard again there were seventy people in our truck – seventy people with all their baggage and not a spare inch in which to move.

The truck was about the same size as the one we had left, the doors slid in a similar way, but now we had four windows, two on each side. The iron bars at the window were placed just wide enough apart for us to get our heads through, and as the train went round bends I could see the other cattle trucks stretching way out behind. We were about halfway along the train and in truck number nineteen. There were about forty trucks in all and every one was packed with poor unfortunates like ourselves, families from all over eastern Poland, whose fathers and husbands had been thrown into prison.

No one knew where we were going; we could only watch the sun to see if we were going north or south. If we went north we thought of Arkhangelsk or the dreaded Nightingale Islands, north of the Arctic Circle. But now we were heading south-east from Sarny, and could only try to forget the stories we had heard of the cold, damp, disease-ridden forest camps of Arkhangelsk on the White Sea.

For three days we slowly went towards the south-east, the train stopping for long periods all the way. Already the heat was almost unbearable, there was not enough ventilation from the tiny windows as we crossed the Russian plains. Mile after mile of small hills and desert-like land passed as the heat increased.

One of the sliding doors in the truck was opened slightly and fixed with a hook, a board with a hole in it was wedged in the opening and this served as our only lavatory. The old people would sit there covering their heads, hoping nobody would look, but there were many young men and women like Jurek and me, who would wait until it was dark before going to the opening. Alongside it children and old people were lying and we had to step over them as we made our way to the board. So tightly was the truck packed that there was no space elsewhere.

During the three-day journey from Sarny to Kiev we were given nothing to eat or drink. At each stop, when the door was pulled open, I was waiting to jump out, but each time we were told there was nothing for us. Food and water would come later when things were better organized, we were told. We pleaded for milk for the baby Barbara, but there was none and the child cried more and more. At first her mother had bent over her to keep her warm, but now it was so hot and there was nothing we could give her.

Many of us crowded to the tiny windows whenever a town

was seen, and there was a great shout as Kiev came into view on our left. We stopped in a siding just outside the city and the guard ordered four of us from the truck to collect food.

By the side of the track stood a roughly erected kitchen and we lined up as two men filled buckets. Our spirits had risen at the talk of food, but when the four of us got back they sank just as quickly; all the buckets contained was a thick and rough barley hash, something like porridge. And the four buckets had to be shared among the seventy people in the truck.

We stayed near Kiev for only half an hour, but the guard agreed to leave the door open and I wandered up the train looking into other trucks for anyone I knew. Every truck was packed like ours; many of the people lay exhausted in the heat and some were already ill. We moved off in an easterly direction and it grew hotter as we went.

The next day was the feast of the Passover and the Jewish family in our wagon began to pray. Everyone in the truck joined in; amid the clatter of the wheels over the endless lines we prayed as we seldom had prayed before, and no one was ashamed. In the truck behind was a Greek Orthodox priest and he must have heard us praying, for later that day we heard his voice, loud and clear, preaching a sermon and we heard the poor wretches in his wagon lift their voices in prayer even as we had done.

For two more days we rumbled eastwards until we halted just outside Kharkov, 250 miles from Kiev. There we were given bread made from sweetcorn, hard and tasteless and impossible to cut. The only way we could eat it was to soak it in water. Jurek was soaking some of his bread when he saw our step-mother trying to eat hers in its dry and hard state. He must have softened towards the woman in that moment and he passed her his water. Then he turned to me and almost apologized. 'I had to help her,' he whispered. 'After all, she is the wife of our father and Henryk is our father's son.'

From then on we gave what food we could spare to our stepmother and Henryk; we still had some left from that given us by the priest's wife. The raw meat was keeping well in salt and the cooked pig's fat would keep for a long time yet. And we watched as our stepmother broke up what we gave her and handed pieces to her own parents. It was not long before our own stocks of food began to disappear and we had nothing but the horrible rations given us by the Russians. Then as we were nearing Kharkov, an old woman vomited and soon practically everyone in the truck was struck with the same excruciating illness.

With the sickness came diarrhoea. In every corner of the truck someone was lying groaning and at times there were almost open fights over the piece of wood jammed in the open door. We were filthy, the air was foul, the stench was horrible. Outside Kharkov a Russian woman railway worker came slowly along the train, tapping the wheels and examining the axles. She wore a dark blue, roughly-cut blouse and black trousers; her face was dark and leathery, but she looked up and smiled as she came to our truck. Just at that moment Jurek threw a piece of the horrible yellow bread through one of the windows. He did not mean to throw it to the woman; I doubt if he even realized she was there, but she saw the bread and pounced on it, and began to eat it ravenously. People from other trucks saw this and threw out more pieces of food, which the woman grabbed and thrust into her mouth. She must have been starving.

We spoke to her and asked if she knew where we were going. She did not, but said: 'Day after day the trains pass, packed like this one with people like yourselves. They come regularly every two hours.' That night, in the darkness of the truck, I thought over the woman's words. I was trying to visualize the magnitude of the disaster which had overtaken eastern Poland.

Next morning, near the siding where we were parked, I saw a small group of peasants and jumped from the truck and ran to them. 'We need milk for the children,' I told them. Baby Barbara was now so ill that we feared for her life. Other children, too, were falling sick because of the complete absence of milk.

The Russians were kind. I could hardly believe it at first, but they had milk with them and gladly gave us some. 'We know you have no milk,' one of the peasants told me. 'It is the same on every train which pulls in here; the children are sick.' Then he said something which showed the sympathy the Russian peasants had for us. 'Wherever you stop,' he said, 'watch for people like us standing near. All along the line you will find us ready to give milk for the little ones.'

The baby was quieter that night. Her tiny stomach at last had the food it needed. But she was still ill; her temperature was rising, and her mother was almost beside herself with worry.

From Kharkov we set off again, almost due north, and again we feared our destination was the malaria-ridden White Sea area. All day we watched the sun, hoping, praying that we would change direction but we still went steadily north. Many times we stopped, but always in open country. The line was a single track and each time a train approached from the north we were drawn into a siding to wait for it to pass. Again the peasants were waiting to help us, but now they were helping openly. They would come right up to the train with their gifts of water, milk, bread and sometimes a little sausage. They could only tell us of the next towns along the line, Kursk and then Orel, but they could not tell us the towns after that. At Orel we could branch eastwards or carry on north to Moscow and north, hundreds of miles north, to Arkhangelsk.

North we crept for two days, past Kursk and still north; we reached Orel, 250 miles from Kharkov and stopped a mile or two from the city. We were praying now that the train would turn eastwards and early the next morning our prayer was answered. Backwards and forwards we were shunted until eventually we turned on to a side line. No one dare say a word as we watched the sun. For over an hour there was hardly a sound, apart from the wheels on the rails and softly murmured prayers. Then suddenly a cheer broke out and spread from truck to truck. We were going east, to what we did not know; but we did not care, provided we were not going north.

On the second day from Orel the train had stopped at a siding and we heard screams from the truck in front. The officer in charge of the guards was called, a big, dark young man with a beautifully waisted tunic, an arrogant man who sang and whistled all day, who ate his ample rations with great relish and laughed at us as we begged scraps from the peasants. He knew where we were going but would never tell us.

A woman was having a baby in the next truck, the officer was told, and the people implored him to find a doctor from the village we could see a mile away. He ordered the people back into the truck. 'A doctor will come,' he said roughly, but the screams went on for another hour. Again they pleaded. This time he was annoyed as he shouted: 'I told you a doctor will come.' For another two hours we heard the screams until eventually the baby was delivered by the other women in the truck. The doctor never came; the officer had not sent for him, but the baby lived.

The towns slowly slipped by – Penza, Syzran – and we turned north-east at Kuibyshev. For days we saw nothing but open, empty countryside. The heat entered the truck as a hot blast. We were growing weaker and weaker as the food became scarcer. On the tenth day from Orel a shout went up and those of us that could pressed to the windows. Ahead of us we could see a large town with factories and tall chimneys cluttering its skyline. Beyond the town we could see the mountains, not tall and peaky but flat, long mountains of brown stone rising to a layer of snow at the top. Here and there on the almost barren slopes were tiny woods, but not the rich, green woods of Poland, just straggly clumps of trees, almost as barren as the brown slopes around them.

We were looking at the town of Zlatoust and beyond it the Ural mountains, the only range we could meet in that easterly direction. We were at the physical boundary of Europe, the boundary which so many had passed and so many more were to pass, never to return.

Through the Urals we climbed into Asia; we had been over two weeks on the journey and had travelled well over two thousand miles since we left Rovno. How much farther were they taking us, how much longer could we live in these conditions? Where for us was the end of the line?

Soon we had crossed the Urals, and when we stopped for water I asked one of the guards where we were going. For the first time we were given some definite information. 'Petropavlovsk,' came the answer as the guard walked on. We quickly scanned the only map we had among us. It was from my school atlas, on a very small scale, with the whole of Europe, Russia and Asia to the Pacific Ocean. We found the Urals, we found Zlatoust, but nowhere could we find Petropavlovsk.

Suddenly Jurek shouted as he stabbed his finger at the map. There was the only Petropavlovsk, but it was Petropavlovsk

Kamchatka, on the extreme eastern coastline of the Soviet Union, north of Japan.

Our hearts sank, it was thousands of miles and weeks and weeks away. If Petropavlovsk Kamchatka was our destination, many of us would not live to reach it. I had a wretched feeling in my stomach. I wanted to be sick. I knew most of us would starve to death on the journey if illness or the heat did not kill us. I looked at the baby Barbara, crying, though softly now, no longer able to scream.

The train trudged on and the following day the baby fell into a coma. The weather was unbearably hot, but her mother kept her covered as she lay on the floor of the truck. By now we were sure that the baby was dying, but there was nothing anyone could do to help. The mother of the Jewish family began to pray and we all joined in. In Polish, in Ukrainian, in Yiddish we prayed for the baby to be spared, and for a time we completely forgot our own plight.

At the end of the day the train stopped in a siding beyond the Urals. The guards shouted to us to collect food and, with two Ukrainian boys, I jumped from the truck. In a line, two or three from each truck, we walked towards the platform and waited for the porridge-like mass, and more of the hard, tasteless, yellow bread.

It was as I was standing in the queue that I became aware of a young man who must have edged up the queue. I realized that I had seen him at other stops, travelling in a truck about three behind ours. He was tall and blond; his face had an arrogant expression and dimly I knew that I had disliked him. He wore Polish cavalry trousers, riding boots and a blazer and I edged away as he spoke. 'Where are you from?' he asked, but I did not reply. I now knew that my dislike was real. I was shy, too, and when he asked the question again it was the Ukrainian boys who answered for me. He grinned at me as he was with his family and they were from Korets, a town on the Polish–Russian border. And gave his name as Kazik Wasilewski.

The conversation ended, but the following day, when the train stopped, I saw him again. As before, he edged along the queue until he was close to me; he was grinning again as my eyes caught his, but I turned away quickly before he could open a conversation. Like many Polish soldiers he appeared to be very sure of himself where women were concerned; I had seen this in our villages during the summer manœuvres. I told myself that I would avoid him from then on.

During the second day we jolted to a halt of two hours, near a town of which we did not know the name. Suddenly, from the front of the train a shout arose. At the side of the line was a signboard with a single word 'Petropavlovsk', and we fell on our knees in prayer. This was the Petropavlovsk we had known nothing about, the one which was not shown on the school atlas. If this was our destination we could survive and the prayers changed into cheers. Even Jasiek, father of baby Barbara, was smiling now; at least there was hope, but from the baby came not a sound.

Soon after the train had started again we came to a junction and saw the sign, 'Moscow – Vladivostock'. It was the main line across Siberia, but as we turned off and saw the sun continuously on our right, we knew we were heading south.

By early morning we came to yet another halt, and we called to the guard for a doctor. His answer told us that we were nearly at the end of the journey. 'It will not be long now,' he shouted back. 'Soon you will be at your destination and there will be a doctor.'

Late that afternoon our hell-train ground to the last halt with its human cargo.[1] It was the end of the line, the terminus. But not in a town as we had expected, for around us was nothing but barren country with grass just bursting out of the greyish-brown, dusty earth. Not a tree, not a bush was to be seen, not a house, not a building.

Dozens of internal security guards were waiting as we stopped, and they began immediately to pull our luggage out of the trucks and throw it to the side of the line. They shouted to the young men and women among us to help and hurried us with shouts that the train had to be turned round to make way for the next one, which was not far behind.

It could have been no more than half an hour before the truck was empty and within another few minutes the train began to chug its way out of sight, bound, no doubt, back to Poland

[1] It was now April 28th.

and later another journey east. We sat on our baggage at the side of the line, hundreds of us wondering what was to be our fate now.

A guard passed and we called to him, 'Where are we?' He did not stop, he did not even turn his head as he hurried past.

CHAPTER III

The Summer of a Siberian Slave

As soon as we had unloaded Jasiek found a commissar and pleaded with him for help for the baby. 'She is dying,' Jasiek told him with tears in his eyes. 'Please, please find a doctor quickly.'

The commissar promised to do what he could, but it was three hours later, at six o'clock, when a small lorry arrived to take baby Barbara and her mother away. By now she was scarcely breathing; her eyes were shut tight and we wept as she was lifted into the lorry.

Soon afterwards more and bigger lorries arrived; they were open and the order was given to load. Those who had strong, grown children had been able to bring large trunks of belongings, sewing machines and plenty of clothes, but others had practically nothing. For hour after hour the loading went on and the lorries were filled with small groups of people perched on top of motley collections of trunks, cases, sewing machines, pots, pans and bundles. We were at the end of the line and we sat watching as the crowd and the mass of baggage got smaller and smaller.

We gathered that the first to be taken in the lorries were going to villages near by, the later ones to villages farther away. When it came to our turn to load, Jasiek asked the commissar how far we were going, and when he replied that it would be about twenty-five miles, Jasiek pleaded to stay near his wife and baby. He told the commissar that the baby was dying and the commissar promised to help.

He kept his word; at ten o'clock our lorry was loaded and on top of the baggage and mattresses sat my stepmother, stepbrother, stepmother's parents, the old aunt, Jasiek, Jurek and I. It was dark now and the nights were as cold as the days were hot. Off into the darkness and cold we went; not a light could be seen, and we huddled as low as we could to escape the freezing wind.

In half an hour or so we came to a village, but it was so dark that there was little we could distinguish. On either side of us I could just see small, low houses; we drove past dozens of them along a straight road and finally came to a stop outside a large building which stood alone. Like most Siberian buildings, it was built of bricks of compressed straw and clay, each two feet square and covered with a lime wash; it was single-storeyed, but its tiled roof was quite high. Later we found that it was the village centre; it had three big rooms which were used as schoolrooms, a library and a recreation room. To us that night it meant nothing more than a place to rest. We were ordered to unload and we carried everything into the front room, which was long and passage-like. The electric lights shone on a mass of people and their belongings.

At once we began to arrange our mattresses in what space we could find and I was bending over my mattress when someone touched my arm. I turned to see a tall, well-built blonde woman about twenty-eight years of age; her eyes were blue and her face was beautiful. She asked if she could help and inquired immediately about the baby.

'I am Gunia Kupuc,' she said. 'I know your father well. My home is at Horodyszcze and I am married to a Polish officer who has been sent to prison.' I had seen the woman occasionally during the train journey, but this was the first time we had spoken. She sat with me for a while on the mattress and as she rose to go she took my hand, 'Don't worry,' she said, 'everything will get better. One day we will get out of this.'

Gunia had walked only a few yards down the passage-like room when I saw someone stop her. It was the tall blond Pole who had tried to speak with me in the queue, Kazik Wasilewski, and I saw him look over to me as he spoke to Gunia.

'Who is your friend?' he asked her and Gunia told him that I was the daughter of a landowner who lived near her village in the Ukraine. 'Would you introduce me?' asked Kazik, and I saw Gunia laugh as she replied, 'If you want to meet Eugenia, introduce yourself. I will not do it for you.'

I saw the arrogant look on his face as Kazik came over to me. He offered his hand, smiled and said: 'Good evening, my name is Kazik Wasilewski. We have a fire, would you care to come and warm yourself?'

I did not know what to say. Although I felt I did not like the man, my heart began to beat faster and I knew that something new, something vague but thrilling, was going on inside me. I took his hand and opened my mouth to speak, but no words came. It seemed minutes that I stood but it could not have been for more than a second or two before Jurek jumped up from where he was sitting on a mattress.

Jurek was annoyed. 'My sister is with us, her family,' he told Kazik. 'She will stay with us. If you have a fire, please go and warm yourself.' Kazik Wasilewski bowed, a short, sharp military bow, then turned smartly on his heel and walked away without a word. He was still smiling at me as he turned.

I felt pleased then that Jurek had intervened, but I watched as Kazik went back to a group of young men. Then all at once I turned away to arrange my mattress for the night. I knew I was blushing with embarrassment, for the men were all grinning at me across the room.

At eleven o'clock a guard put out the lights. There must have been over thirty families in the building, over a hundred people, and the conditions were cramped. In the darkness we began to pray, and our voices rose as those in the other rooms joined in. We broke into hymns and Polish religious songs, until gradually the whole building quietened and soft snoring took the place of the singing. For those who had no mattresses even the hard wooden boards were a cosy bed after the interminable nights on the train.

Early the next morning a commissar came into the building and we all stood as he jumped on to a table to shout at us in Polish. 'This is the village where you will stay,' he said. 'You must go out and find yourselves somewhere to live. You cannot stay in this building. It is used as a school to teach the Russian way of life, the right Communist thinking.'

From all around me came the shouts: 'We did not want to come here. Why should we find a place to live? You brought us here, now you must look after us.'

The commissar stamped his foot and shouted for order. 'We did not bring you here, we do not know why you were sent,' he said. 'All we know is that now you are here we must see that you work. Behave yourselves and do not sabotage the Communist way of life or break the law. You are free to move about the village or anywhere within a radius of fifty miles. There are farms to work on – and if you want to live you will have to work.'

It was useless to argue and we were quiet as the commissar continued. 'When you work you will be paid and given corn to make bread,' he said. 'You must settle down in the community. You will be treated exactly the same as the others here. Now each of you is one of us.' I did not know then, but for the whole time I stayed in Siberia I was not to be paid a single rouble for all the work I did.

We gathered up our belongings and carried them outside the building, every move being watched by a crowd of women and children who had come to see who the new arrivals were. They were still in their winter clothes, the women in thick cotton skirts and blouses or dresses and each of them wearing two scarves, one white and across the forehead, the other coloured and pulled down the head, crossed under the chin and tied behind the neck. The women wore boots, thick, black felt boots pressed into the shape of the feet, but most of the children were barefooted. They all wore coats, three-quarter length and drab, but wadded for warmth. They stood looking at us as though we were from another world; not one of them spoke, not one of them smiled.

I looked to my left and down the village street, wide and straight with houses on either side, all equally spaced. The houses were identical and the village was modern for that part of Russia. Each house was built half into the ground and steep steps led down to the entrance; above the ground the house was only a few feet high and two tiny, fixed windows were set in the front walls. The roofs were made from one long centre beam of wood running the length of the house, with smaller and thinner joists falling to the sides, which were covered first with thick rushes and then with a layer of mixed clay and ox blood to make it rainproof. The walls were like those of the building in which we had slept: straw and clay compressed into bricks and held together with more clay.

Each house had a garden, but nowhere could I see flowers; in most of the gardens there were potatoes or the sweetcorn which never seemed to ripen and could be eaten only as a boiled hash. Each house had its well: wooden boards forming a square hole with a block of wood across the top and a chain and bucket attached. The water I hated from the first day; it was always salty.

As I found later, each house was about fifty feet long and some were built as one huge room while others were divided into two. The floors were of clay and at one end, if they had not built a tiny separate kitchen, stood the stove, brick-sided, about two feet high and across the top rested the metal cooking plate. The stove was placed so that the heat rose into the walls and roof and kept the house warm in winter; the only fuels to be had were straw and dried manure, stamped out flat and cut into bricks.

Beds were plain wooden boards arranged near the fire or warm walls. Some were lucky enough to have straw-filled mattresses, but nobody undressed for sleeping; they just took off their boots and used their topcoats as covering, together with the one or two blankets they possessed.

Each house had a stable in which were kept a cow and a pig. To keep the animals warm in winter the stable was built into the house and the only way into the rooms was through the stable. In summer the flies came into the stables in their hundreds and overflowed into the rooms, and the smells were almost unbearable.

In the centre of the village were three bungalow-type buildings which were different from the rest. They were not built into the ground; they had wooden floors, tiled roofs and were kept very clean. In one lived and worked the head of the village, who was registrar of births, deaths, marriages and was the judge when anyone broke the local laws. The second was a school for the village children and the third was the house of the manager of the farms attached to the village. There were three farms which had to be worked by the village, and according to where you lived in the village you were sent to one of the three farms.

The inhabitants, I found, were mostly Russian, sent there by the Czar in 1910 with enough materials and cattle to make a start. Most of them came from the Moscow area, but there were Poles and Ukrainians too, who had been forced, like us, into Siberia in 1935 and 1936 when the Russians cleared them from where they lived near the Polish border. The population was about two thousand. All the roads criss-crossed, cutting it into perfect squares and the gardens of the houses backed on to each other with roads between. The farm buildings were left from when they were owned by wealthy landowners who had been dispossessed.

At the bottom of the village ran a river and I was told later of the people who had lived on the other side many years before. They were of the Khirgiz tribe, small, broad men with legs bent from horse-riding, slit eyes like Japanese, and brown skins. Remains of what they had left I could see across the river and I was told that they lived in the open on the steppes gathering their sheep and cattle around huge fires at night to keep the wolves away.

When the Russians came they had tried to make the Khirgiz work on the land, but the Khirgiz had refused. Instead they had gradually moved away to Mongolia and later I saw many of the villages they left, with houses similar to ours but with black walls, in which the women and children of the tribe had lived whilst the men tended their herds out on the steppes. Now the villages were derelict and crumbling into ruins.

The nearest village across the river had been called Pryreczno, and as we stood outside the club building with our baggage, that first morning in Siberia, we learned that the name of the village which was to be our home was Novo Pryreczno, 'novo' meaning 'new'.

It was some time before the village women spoke, but we saw that they were studying our clothes. True, these were old, dirty or crumpled from our long journey, but to the women of Novo Pryreczno, in their rough home-made clothes, they looked modern and well made. And it was our clothes that broke the barrier between us, for soon the women were asking where we had come from and why we had been sent there. Then quickly they turned the conversations to our clothes and were offering to buy them.

In exchange they offered corn, potatoes and milk, and as soon as we heard the word 'milk' the bartering started. I sold a pair of stockings, some underwear and a dress and was given a large can of milk, some corn and potatoes. On that first day I discovered that I would have to barter to live and I carefully guarded every tiny thing I had brought with me.

We asked the women where we could live, but found that the younger ones would not offer us shelter. They had families of their own and their houses were full, so our only hope was to find newly-married couples or old people who had more space in their houses. Jurek and I were told of a house at the far end of the village where lived an elderly couple and their daughter. My stepmother was told of another house near by and we picked up our belongings and walked there.

Our reception was not warm, but the woman finally agreed to let Jurek and me stay. She was Russian, her husband worked on one of the farms and she was now too old to look after the cows as she had done for years. Her daughter was a railway worker and we found that she worked at the terminus where we had been detrained the day before.

The house was of the single-room type with a kitchen and the stable in which were kept a cow and a pig, and we moved our belongings in. In one corner was our bed of hard wooden boards, and I saw the open-eyed wonderment on the faces of the family as I unpacked our mattress, pillows and blankets. Never before had the family seen such comfort and I looked at the rags they had for blankets. I offered them one of my blankets and there were tears in the eyes of the sixty-year-old mother as she took it and put it to her face as though she were caressing it. Then she put her arms around me and thanked me a dozen times. Jurek and I were accepted; we were among friends from then on.

There was room for only the one bed for us both and we arranged it so that Jurek got in one end and I got in the other, sleeping head to feet.

In the evening we went to find food; there was enough in the

house only for the Russian family and we found that they could
not even spare us a little milk from the cow, so much of it had to
be given up to the farm. When they killed the pig, they told us,
they were allowed to keep only half and the skin was exchanged
for shoes. But sometimes, said the woman, there was not enough
skin from a pig for a whole pair of shoes or boots in one year.
Then they would have to wait until the following year, when
another pig was killed, before they could have one pair between
the three of them.

Jurek and I walked down the village street until we came to a
small building which was known as the shop. But even before we
reached it we knew our journey had been wasted; the shop was
closed because it had nothing to sell. At times, the villagers told
us, they would hear that something would be on sale at the
shop the following day. They would line up from the early hours
of the morning, but seldom could they buy more than a tiny bar
of soap or a piece of chocolate. And never did they know what
would be for sale when they queued.

Only once did I join the queue, but what there was for sale
was almost useless and I had wasted hours. If we wanted something we had to barter; this was the only way we could exist.
That evening we bartered a few small articles of clothing for
some milk and white flour. For the first few months we found
this was fairly easy, but we could never buy or barter for vegetables.

On the way back we called at the house where my stepmother
was living. She had found a young Russian couple who had a
tiny baby and had just enough room to take her, her son and
Jasiek. Jasiek had been at the hospital all that day and he
arrived soon after us. Barbara was still alive, he told us; an old
Russian doctor was fighting hard to save her life and had given
her injections. Jasiek told us that the hospital was full of young
babies and old people, all terribly ill after the long train ride
from Poland. Then he broke down and cried as he said: 'We
must all go to the hospital tomorrow; it may be the last time
that we shall see the baby alive.'

My stepmother's parents and the old aunt had found a home
with a Russian couple with six children. The parents worked
on the farm, the younger children were put in a kindergarten

and the old people were welcomed when they promised to look after the older children after they left school.

Back at our house that night Jurek and I had a conference with the Russian and his wife. It was agreed that we younger ones would go out to work and the Russian woman would cook for us. She started there and then; with the flour she baked some plain and almost tasteless cakes and we ate them with some of the salted meat we still had in a bucket.

The house was hot, sleep was impossible and I could see that Jurek was restless as he felt among our baggage in the dark corner. Without a word he went to the door of the house and stood outside in the night air. Dreamy Polish music floated back into the house; Jurek had found the only thing he had brought from Rovno – his concertina. The Russians smiled, they liked music, they said, and walked to the door where Jurek stood.

But Jurek played for only about five minutes, for so many young people, mostly Poles, came up the street when they heard the music and started to sing that the Russian woman asked Jurek to stop. She did not like people to gather at her house, she said; she feared trouble from the head of the village and wished to remain quiet and unnoticed. Jurek did not play his concertina again at the house.

It was eleven o'clock and we went to bed. I was tired now and slept well, my second night in Siberia.

Early next morning the whole of our family set off for the town and the hospital. Jasiek knew the way and led us along the clay road covered with tiny pebbles from the river bed, and after an hour's walking we arrived at Novo Sukhotino. I was surprised to find such a large town. First we passed large blocks of two-storeyed houses where the security police, the railwaymen and a host of other officials lived in two-roomed flats. They were built of the same straw and clay bricks, but had tiled roofs and wooden floors. Four families shared a communal kitchen and there were two bathrooms to each block of a dozen or so flats.

Just past the flats we came to the nursery gardens; hundreds of tiny trees had been planted in an attempt to grow species hardy enough to stand the Siberian winters. When they were large enough they would be planted on the steppes into long barriers against the biting wind which tore the seeds from the ground and even tore at the ground itself, it was so strong.

Then we came to the market, but this was very different from any market I had known in Poland. This was an open, barren space. This day was one of the two weekly market days and the place was crammed with people. Some squatted with sacks of flour, bread or meat they wished to sell, while others wandered around with materials, second-hand clothes or blankets draped over their arms. Hundreds of people were feeling the quality of the materials, buying bread or holding dresses against themselves for size.

It seemed to me that everything could be bought at that market, but when I tried later I found that I would need a fortune just for the few things I needed. On the outskirts of the market were pigs and chickens for sale, but never did I have enough money to buy them all the time I was in Siberia.

Farther in we saw many of the people we had known in Poland. Some had been on our train, but many others had come earlier and we found that whenever they could they went to Novo Sukhotino to gather news of friends, of relatives who had come before them or had just arrived. In the days to come, I discovered, it was to be the only news centre in the whole of our area. We even got news of those who had been released from prison back home, and whenever anyone received a letter they took the news to Novo Sukhotino to share it.

Most of the houses in the town were similar to those in Novo Pryreczno, built into the ground. There were hundreds of them. The town had originally been built by the Khirgiz and some of the tribe still lived there. They were easy to distinguish with their long leather boots, fur jackets and fur hats. Their oriental features stood out in sharp contrast with the Russians. And there was the third type of people who lived in the towns; the contrast between them and the Khirgiz or Russians was so great that at first I could not fit them into the scene at all.

They were taller than the rest, with long, thin faces and narrow cheek-bones. Their skin was yellow and they, too, had orientally slit and slanting eyes. But it was their clothes which made me look so hard and long when I first saw them. The men wore smart trousers, black or blue, well-cut jackets and spotlessly clean white shirts with the collars turned out over their jackets. The women were just as smart; their dresses or suits, although home-made, were beautifully fashioned and clean; they wore no head-scarves like the Russian women and looked European dressed, even to their shoes.

That day I did not have time to inquire about them, but I was told later that they were Koreans, that thousands of them had come to Russia in the 1930s and were free to live where they liked. Nearly all of them preferred the steppes to European Russia, because the climate was more like their own and they were nearer their own land. They had complete freedom of movement and could visit any town they wished; they were well-educated and mostly worked in offices or schools. One of them, I found, was a teacher at our village.

On the far outskirts of the town we eventually came to the hospital; long, single-storeyed, square buildings with clean-scrubbed wooden floors. We soon met the doctor, sixtyish, with a long black beard; he wore a neat grey suit and a white jacket, and like doctors I had known at home his stethoscope hung around his neck.

'We are doing everything possible for the baby but she is very ill,' said the doctor. His voice was soft and kindly and he led us to the room where baby Barbara lay. Her mother had been allowed to sleep in the same room. We saw her for a few moments but she was so distraught; nothing we said could comfort her. In the hospital were about a hundred patients, a few of them accident cases from the local city but almost everyone else was a victim of the train journey from Poland.

That night Jurek and I learned more about bartering. We found that for a thimbleful of tiny beads from one of my dresses we could get three eggs. With flour, salt and a little milk the Russian woman where we lived made them into a meal before we went to bed, tired out after our long walk.

The next afternoon baby Barbara came to our village – dead. Jasiek had gone to the hospital early that morning, but the baby had died before he got there. His wife had collapsed. A kindly farmer had given them a lift in a lorry and they arrived with Jasiek holding his dead child wrapped in a blanket.

The villagers were kind to us that day. Somewhere they found some wooden boards for Jasiek to make a tiny coffin with and my stepmother made a long white dress for the dead child. It was late in the evening when we followed Jasiek as he pushed the coffin on a barrow through the village to the cemetery, a wide open space on the steppe without a wall or a fence. Nothing sacred, just stones lying here and there with no regularity, some with a star scratched on them and others with a weird, Buddhist sign which belonged to the Khirgiz tribe who first buried their dead sitting up and returned in six months to wash and rebury the bones.

Jasiek and Jurek dug a hole, baby Barbara was buried and we knelt in prayer beside the grave. There was no priest, not even a church, in our village but the child was given a Christian burial. We left a small wooden cross to mark the grave; it was the only one I could see standing upright. Here and there others were scattered, but they did not appear to belong to any grave in particular. Barbara's mother lay beside the grave during most of the simple ceremony. We carried her home; she was mercifully unconscious.

On the fifth day the farm manager visited Jurek and me. We knew that he could not force us, but he made us understand that if we did not work there would be nothing for us and eventually we must starve.

'If you start work now,' he said, 'at the end of the year you will receive enough wheat, potatoes and money to live all the following year.' It sounded convincing then, but we were soon to discover that there would be precious little reward, however hard we worked. I agreed to start work at the Number One farm the following day, but Jurek decided on Number Two farm. He knew several of the workers there and preferred me to be with them. And he had also heard that his chances were better there for earning money.

At eight o'clock in the morning I climbed aboard the lorry which was to take us to work. There were two other women, one of them the wife of an arrested policeman, Jasiek and myself. We had been told to wear warm clothes for the journey; I had on the fur coat given me by the dentist's wife and a scarf around my head.

For nearly an hour we travelled over the clay and pebble roads across the barren steppes which had hardly a sign of habitation. Finally we stopped in open fields, the lorry drove off and a foreman took charge of us. Our task was to plant tiny trees, and after a demonstration which took no more than a minute we were put to work.

All that day I worked, bending over until I thought my back would break. With a small pointed tool I dug the holes before planting the trees and trod in the earth around them with my foot. But I did not know how to hold the tool properly; I did not grip it firmly enough and within an hour my hands were red and blistered.

We had brought our own food with us that morning: bread, pork fat and milk. But when the time came for a break for food I found that the heat of the sun had turned the milk sour. Some of the women – there were dozens working in the fields – drank their milk sour, but from that day I drank my milk as soon as I arrived. There was nothing else except water from a tank, but this was so brackish that I could not touch it. I preferred to drink the milk fresh, even if it meant nothing else for the rest of the day.

At the end of the first day I was exhausted; I had a permanent stoop and the pains in my back were horrible. The heat of the sun had made my head ache and all I could think of was sleep. That night, when I got back to the house, I was almost too tired to eat.

The following day I was planting trees again, but Jasiek refused to go. Under the Russian system so many planted rows constituted a day's work, but we had not planted enough the day before and had qualified for no pay at all. 'It is too hard,' said Jasiek. 'Never will I earn money at that work. I will find another job.'

I carried on for about two weeks, gradually becoming used to the bending and hard work. My hands became hard like a man's and I was not so tired when I got back to the village at night.

One day a commissar came to the village and Jurek and I went to see him, asking for news of father and reminding him of the promise that we were to join him. The commissar passed his hand across his face to hide a grin. 'I know nothing of a promise,' he said, 'but if you were promised perhaps that is what will happen.'

He grinned again as he turned away and we now knew how we had been tricked. The Russians had lied to us; there was no hope of seeing father, and perhaps we would never see him again. We were trapped.

It was a long time before we heard news of father; it was when we received a letter from a friend of my stepmother who still lived in Rovno. Father had been taken from the jail there, we were told, and was now in a jail at Kiev. Later we heard he had been moved to another jail at Kharkov.

At first, when I worked on the farm, I stayed at home after my evening meal, but one night I persuaded Jurek to take me to see a film which was to be shown at the club, the large building where we had spent our first night in Novo Pryreczno. The film was Communist propaganda, but I enjoyed it for the music and the dancing. It was called 'The Last Gypsy' and told the story of how the gypsy gave up his life of wandering, went to work on a Communist farm and earned so much money that he was able to build a lovely house and live happily ever after.

There were shouts, laughs and whistles from the young Polish boys as the film came to its end, but there was silence immediately the lights were switched on. The head of the village was standing near the screen and his face was livid with anger. 'You will find that this is the truth,' he shouted. 'Long live Soviet Russia.'

That was the only evening I was out after dark in those first three weeks. Jurek was strict and worried what might happen with so many young men around the village. If I spent evenings with my stepmother I was always back in the house before darkness.

At the end of three weeks planting trees, I decided not to work in the fields again. I had not earned one rouble and knew that, however hard I worked, I could not defeat the Russian system of measuring what was supposed to be a day's work. I improved, of course, but each time I planted more rows the foreman told me that the measure had been changed and that I must work harder still. It was hopeless. I was disgusted. I told the foreman one night that I would not go planting again.

That night I was in the house when I heard the sound of music along the street. I went to the door and saw two Russian boys of about twenty walking down the street playing concertinas. The music was gay and they were collecting the young people as they went along; they were off to the club to dance and I longed to go with them.

I begged Jurek to let me go, but at first he refused. He was going to play chess at another house and he said that he would not allow me to be taken by another boy. It was not until two girls, one the sister of Kazik Wasilewski and the other a policeman's daughter, came along that Jurek agreed. I could go with them, he said.

It was not yet seven o'clock when we arrived at the club and I was surprised to see how many people were there. Nearly a hundred, young and old, Polish and Russian, were dancing to the music of the concertinas. I felt strange, but thrilled; for the first time I was out without an escort from my family. But I felt shy, too, and stood in a corner with my two friends.

For a long time we stood watching and then the two boys played a waltz. One of my friends looked at me and asked, 'Shall we dance?' and the two of us took the floor. It was good to dance again and as when we used to dance at school I took the male steps. I might have been back at school at that moment. I was happy for the first time in weeks.

The next dance was a Russian Cossack dance. At first the boys danced along and gradually went down into the squatting position, kicking out their legs in front of them. It was the first time I had seen the Cossack dance and we edged our way nearer and nearer until we were at the front of those watching.

Suddenly the music stopped, a Russian boy jumped up in front of me and clicked his heels. I did not know it but that was an invitation; when that happened the girl was supposed to dance with the boy, if only for a few steps. I looked at the boy; I recognized him as a member of the Communist Youth Movement who went off from the village every day on his bicycle. But I was not thinking of the youth movement or the bicycle just then; I felt terribly shy, dropped my head and hid behind my friends.

Quickly someone behind, a Russian woman, explained that I

must dance, otherwise it would be an insult. My friends gently pushed me forward and I found myself being whirled around by the Russian youth.

I danced for only a few steps, but that was enough, I had done what was expected of me. Afterwards I danced several times with other Russian and Polish boys. I liked this new freedom which, strangely enough, had come to me for the first time while in captivity.

The older Russians were friendly and encouraged us to dance. 'We live together and must all be friends,' they said and they meant it. Their lot was little better than ours. That night I could have been back in Rovno itself, before the Russians came.

My friends took me home before half past ten; they knew that Jurek would be furious if I was late, but Jurek was not at home when I arrived. He played chess and draughts so well, I discovered, that many people in the village would pay him to play with them. He had found a useful source of income. He came home very late when I was asleep, a happy sleep – a contented sleep for the first time in months.

The following day I was offered another job. A Russian woman surveyor had arrived in the village and she needed an assistant who could ride a horse. I took the job; it was to go out on the steppes with the woman, hold the thin pole where she directed whilst she used her theodolite, measured out the land and mapped it.

We went far out on the steppes that day, farther than I had been before. Everywhere was barren and we saw no one else all day. The horse I had to ride was hitched to the wagon as we went out, but when we started work I found myself in difficulties. The horse was not short like the Cossack horses; it was tall and had no saddle. Trying to hold the pole the woman had given me, I clutched the mane of the horse to pull myself up. I must have fallen at least six times before I found a way to keep the horse still and mount it at the same time.

The only way we could keep track of our whereabouts was to listen for the trains. We were somewhere along the line between Petropavlovsk and Karaganda. Coal trains passed every half-hour and we were careful not to get out of earshot. We must have worked our way very many miles from our village before the woman surveyor decided to set out for home, and it was eleven o'clock that night when I reached the house, tired and hungry.

Jurek was furious. He stormed at me for staying out so late, despite the fact that I had been working. 'If papa were here,' shouted Jurek, 'you would not stay out until this hour. You would not dare.' I was annoyed. I shouted back: 'If papa were here I would not have to go out to work. We are equal now; we both work; everybody works. I do not wish to starve.'

We went to bed when the argument finished, but I was crying to myself. The night before had been so happy; now I was unhappy.

I stayed with the woman surveyor for about ten days. I liked riding the horse through the long grass and got to know the tiny animals which rushed about under the horses hooves. There were the field-mice, but big, like rats; there were the vultures, silvery-grey, which hovered above, waiting to pounce on the mice, and I always felt sad as a vulture flew away with one dangling from its beak. There were the hares, about the same size as a European hare, but with long, thin, fluffy-ended, tails. I never knew why they were called hares, for they jumped like kangaroos. They were almost tame; they were my friends.

One day I was riding the horse when it suddenly began to snort. I had nothing to control it with except its mane and soon it was rearing until I was thrown into the long grass. The horse ran away and it was a long walk back to the wagon, but I was unhurt. I was not even worried until I reached the woman surveyor. Then, like her, I became scared. There were wolves near by, she said; she had seen them when the horse panicked. We stopped work at once and made our way back to the village.

On another day we were completely lost on the steppes and decided that the surveyor should wait with the horses whilst I would look for help. For over an hour I walked before I came to a small group of people working in a field, but I did not recognize any of them and found that I was miles from my own village. The workers could only direct me to the nearest village. Here I was given bread and water before setting out again to find the surveyor, and I walked for well over an hour before we met.

D

From one village we were directed to the next. All night we walked and it was daylight before we found our own village. All through the night the horses bucked and reared, and for most of the time it seemed that we were surrounded by tiny distant fires. But these were not fires; they were the eyes of wolves, following us all through the night, waiting to pounce on the horses if we should leave them. It was summer and wolves never attacked human beings in summer. But all animals were kept under close guard at night, all through the year, for wolves attacked them at any time.

The days went by and the heat increased. By day I went out to the steppes with the woman surveyor and sometimes in the evenings I was allowed to go to the club to see a film. Rarely was I allowed there to dance and I wanted to dance so much; I wanted to be with other young people; but Jurek was against it.

I still earned nothing; all I got was the promise that my wages would come later. My money was getting less and less and the clothes that I had brought with me disappeared piece by piece as they were bartered for food and milk. I despaired of the work that seemed fruitless, always for the promise of reward to come later. Although I liked it much better than planting trees, I decided to give it up.

I need not have bothered. On the morning I failed to report I heard that the woman surveyor had been arrested. She had been accused of sabotage. Her measurements of the steppes were wrong, it was said; she was taken away and I never saw her again.

CHAPTER IV

Betrothal and Marriage

A few days later I was sitting alone in the house; Jurek had gone out for the evening and I longed to go out myself. I was bored, I had heard that there was a film being shown that evening at the club, but I knew that Jurek would be annoyed if I went without his permission. I was feeling rebellious. Why, I thought, could I not be free to do as I wished? I worked as hard as Jurek, as hard as any of the men. And had I not been told that in Russia we were all equals, men and women?

I knew that Jurek would not be home until late, and suddenly I made up my mind. I would go to the club, whatever Jurek said later. Through the village to the club I hurried and reached there just before the lights went out for the beginning of the film. I felt nervous at being alone among the other people, but I felt defiant too.

The film was propaganda, of course, but as I thought of it later I could not have seen a film which fitted more into the events of that evening. It told the story of a Russian girl who worked on a farm and a boy who worked on the railway. Every day his train passed the field where the girl worked and they smiled and waved to each other. One day, with stones, the girl spelt out the words 'I love you' in the field before the train passed; the boy saw them, they married, worked hard for the Soviet State and lived happily ever after.

It was a stupid story, but for two hours my mind was far away from the village of Novo Pryreczno and when the film finished I hardly realized where I was. Then someone took my arm and I heard the whispered words, 'May I take you home?'

Tall, blond Kazik Wasilewski stood beside me. He was smiling down at me and I found myself replying 'Yes' immediately. We walked slowly through the darkened village towards my house, and Kazik gently held my arm. He asked me where my home was in Poland, and who were my parents. I was sure that he knew the answers, for he had asked all the questions before. But it did not seem to matter.

Outside my house we stopped; Kazik held both my hands in his. Suddenly I was pulled towards him, his arms were around me, he was kissing me and I was not objecting. It was the first time I had ever been kissed by a stranger and the first time I had been kissed like that. And I knew I was liking it.

Inside me everything seemed on fire. I was in a daze; I could not resist. Kazik was whispering into my ear. I felt his hot breath close to me and he kissed my hair. 'Will you marry me?' he asked. I heard the words and quickly the thoughts pounded through my mind. I had been kissed; surely this meant I should marry the man? It would mean freedom – freedom from Jurek and freedom to do as I wished.

Kazik was asking me the question again, but now I knew what my answer must be. 'Yes,' I whispered and he kissed me again. I was still close to him as he murmured that he would see my stepmother to ask her permission. Then I broke away and ran into the house. Jurek was not home. I went to bed, but my head was in a whirl. For an hour I lay, thrilled then frightened, until at last I slept.[1]

I said nothing to Jurek next morning, but in the evening he came home in a furious temper: somebody had told him that I had been brought home by a man; he did not know who it was, but he was shouting at me: 'If I find you alone with any man again I will break his head.'

For the first time I laughed at Jurek's temper. 'You can do nothing now,' I answered him defiantly. 'I am going to be married.'

Jurek gasped. His face made me laugh again. 'Never, never!' he cried. 'You will not get married until you get permission, and papa is not here to give permission.'

Now I was furious: how dare he try to stop me getting married? 'Under Russian law I shall be free to marry next week,' I shouted. 'You will not stop me, nobody will stop me now.'

[1] I was betrothed on May 24th.

In a few days I would be eighteen and Jurek quickly realized this. But he was still shouting as he left the house to go to my stepmother. 'You will never marry,' I heard him scream. 'I will stop it, I will stop it.'

A few days later Kazik went to my stepmother to ask permission. She pointed out that this should come from my father, but in the circumstances she considered that she was the next in the family to give permission, and she gave it.

Jurek would not agree. We argued for days until eventually I asked my stepmother if I could go to live with her. Then Jurek went to see Kazik to tell him that I would not make a good wife. He said that I was too young to marry and did not know my own mind. He even tried to dissuade Kazik by telling him that I could not cook. But Kazik would not listen.

Still Jurek did not give up. He came to me daily, arguing at first, then pleading. He told me that I was pig-headed, too young, that Kazik's blond hair and good looks were the only things that attracted me. He was sure I would not stay with Kazik, and finally begged me not to marry a Pole. 'If you marry a Pole under our religion,' said Jurek, 'it is something sacred. You marry for ever. If you were marrying a Russian under Russian laws it would be so much easier. You could end the marriage at any time.'

Perhaps I knew that what Jurek was telling me was true, but I would not admit that I was pig-headed and I would listen no more. At last Jurek gave me up, but he still tried to talk Kazik out of the marriage.

For the next few weeks I saw Kazik often, but never alone. I saw him as he worked in the fields or on the farm, always singing, always happy. I went to the village club with Kazik's sisters, Christina and Czesia, and visited his mother, a small and kindly woman and mother of a large family. I met Kazik's father, a forester from Poland, and his three younger brothers. Gradually I became accepted as one of the family. They had a house to themselves and more food than most of us in the village, for many parcels were sent by relatives in Poland and there was always food for me when I visited the house. My family had so little that I would almost have starved but for Kazik's mother.

·   ·   ·   ·   ·

In June we were ordered to do haymaking, so thirty of us went from the village in two lorries and I was pleased to see Jurek among the working party. I had seen little of him during the past weeks, and I had missed him. Perhaps I was not sure that I liked Kazik, but I dared not admit it. I wanted freedom, but did not know quite how to get it, except through marriage.

We travelled over forty miles from the village for the haymaking and on the way we stopped at one of the few remaining Khirgiz villages with houses like our own, but with walls of black clay. The younger women were beautiful, dressed in colourful clothes, yellows, oranges and reds, which set off their olive skins. Their dresses were mostly of damask with mandarin collars, the buttons were set with bright stones, and sometimes the buttons were of pure gold.

The Khirgiz could never be persuaded to work in the fields with us. They were allowed to keep their beautiful cossack horses and each year the Russians gave them corn to sow. And each year they used the corn to make bread and told the Russians that they had sown the corn but it had not grown.

After a few days haymaking we were put to roadmaking and I was given a cart with two oxen to collect gravel from the river bed. We all had to load our own carts, hard and back-breaking work. The oxen I was given were weak from lack of food; they could hardly pull the cart and sometimes fell or sat down under the strain. It was no use pulling them, but I found a way of making them move: if they sat down I would scare them with an Indian-style war-cry. The oxen did not like it; they always jumped up at once and sometimes even ran.

The roadmaking lasted nearly a week and Jurek and Jasiek worked with me. One day Jurek produced a small board and a set of draughts; the oxen were travelling slowly and we sat on the top of the gravel playing the game. For a long time we did not notice the car behind us; the oxen strayed all over the road and the car driver was furious by the time he was able to pass.

That night we discovered who he was – a Russian commissar – and soon the head of our village sent for us. He threatened us for holding up the commissar and warned us that if the carts were damaged through our negligence money would be stopped from our wages to pay for the damage. We laughed as we left the office, for none of us had received any pay until then; it was promised at the end of the year when all the crops were gathered in and sold. The only wages we had had until now were the occasional tickets we could beg from the head of the village which allowed us a meagre portion of flour to make bread.

Soon we had to find other ways of working for food, and some of us offered to work for our Russian neighbours. The men had to work on the farms and they had little time to look after their own vegetable gardens. We worked for anything so long as it was something to eat; sometimes we worked all day for a tiny piece of butter and a can of milk. The Russians could afford no more, we knew, but it often kept us from days of starvation.

By now the weather had become stifling hot. We all slept in one large bed at my stepmother's house and the heat, the smell of the cow and the pig made the nights unbearable. I decided to sleep outside the house, but I got little more sleep there, for our Russian neighbours sang all night because they could not sleep, the same monotonous tune to the music of a balalaika. Every night it was the same tune, only the words, composed spontaneously by the Russians, broke the monotony.

Came the day of my wedding,[1] it was two o'clock when we went to the office for the ceremony, Kazik, his sister Czesia and myself. And it was four minutes later that I walked out a wife, a few papers signed in a ceremony which was no more impressive than the sale of a cow or an ox. We walked back to Kazik's house and I felt unchanged. Was this the wedding day I had sometimes dreamed of as a child?

The reception lasted for three hours. Kazik's arms were always around me and gradually I found that I was afraid of him. I was not used to drinking, but as the fear of what I had done mounted in my mind I drank more and more vodka. I staggered and eventually lost consciousness. I must have been carried to the nearby house where we had found a room, for I knew nothing more until the following morning. When I awoke I saw the small religious picture which hung over the bed; Kazik was beside me but fast asleep. My head was throbbing

[1] July 28th.

and I felt giddy. I quietly left the bed without waking Kazik and went to work in the fields to dig potatoes.

All day I felt a strange sense of fear, something which was not clear in my mind, I dreaded the approach of evening when I would have to go home to Kazik.

I stayed with Kazik only that night. I knew now of what I was afraid: I had been taught nothing of the normal facts of life and I hated Kazik. I thought he was cruel and inhuman. I realized that I hated marriage as much as I hated Kazik.

The next morning I went to my mother-in-law and told her that I was leaving Kazik. She listened but there was little need for me to explain. Kazik's mother understood. She asked if I would like to stay with her – as 'her own daughter' – but I said I would rather go back to my stepmother. Stepmother tried to persuade me to return to Kazik; now that I was married, she said, I was his. But nothing could make me change my mind and eventually she agreed that I could stay with her.

Even Jurek tried to persuade me to go back to Kazik. We were Poles, he said, whatever I felt, and my place was with my husband. Although we had married in Siberia he still felt that the laws of our own religion bound us.

That day I went to work as usual and the same evening Kazik came to my stepmother to plead with her for my return, to no avail. Kazik went away alone, only to return the following day with small gifts of food and a few wild flowers he had picked in the fields. I ordered him from the house and threw the flowers after him. I told him never to visit me again.

It was many months before I returned to Kazik, but for a long time he visited me once or twice a week. Finally he gave up and then tried to make me jealous. Free to go out now when I wished, I often visited the club and if Kazik was there he would dance with other girls. If he thought I was noticing, he would kiss them, but he failed to make me jealous. I gradually lost my hatred of him; I was trying to forget.

Often I saw Kazik in the fields as he worked, and sometimes he would sing Russian and Polish love songs at the top of his voice, trying to annoy me. I still visited his mother; she was always kind to me, but I tried not to visit her when Kazik was at home.

Gradually I made new friends at the club now that I was free to go out alone. At first the Russians had not liked us, they looked on us as a different type of people; now they were accepting us and most of them were friendly. Many times I danced with the Russian boys and they loved to teach me the Russian dances and learn Polish ones from me.

One evening I was visiting Kazik's mother when I recognized the woman who lived in the next house. She was Gunia Kupuc, the woman who had spoken to me that first night in Siberia, and she asked me in. For the first time since I had left Poland I had found a real friend. Gunia was several years older, but she was someone I could talk to at last, could confide in.

She was very different from the other women. Not since the day we had arrived at Novo Pryreczno had she worked for the Russians, for she had brought with her nearly all her husband's possessions. He had been a Polish officer; prices were high for men's clothing and Gunia was living very well by selling his uniforms and riding boots piece by piece.

From eastern Poland and also the German-occupied part of west Poland Gunia received occasional food parcels and always she seemed to have the latest news from Europe. She was living in more comfort than any other Poles in the village in a house she shared with a couple of Polish origin who had been sent to Siberia in 1936. Gunia had a bed and small pieces of furniture such as I had not seen elsewhere.

She told me that I had been silly to marry. 'You are too young,' she said. 'You had plenty of time to marry and I am sure you will not be happy when the war ends and you have to go back to Poland with Kazik.' Gunia had taught at a school in the village where Kazik had lived and she knew the family well; it would be a poor life there, said Gunia, nothing like what I had been used to.

The weather was still hot, suffocating and dirty, and my next job was at the farm which ran down to the river. The Russians were trying to grow cabbages, cucumber and water-melons and had planned an irrigation scheme; large trenches were dug across the fields, pipes were to be laid in them and pumps would be used to get the water from the river. But like so many other Russian schemes this was not working out so simply. The pipes arrived but the pumps did not; somewhere else, where they had the same scheme, the pumps had arrived but the pipes had not. So it was decided that we must get along without the pumps.

Most of us from the village who did not have other jobs were pressed into this one; even my stepmother, who had not worked before, was told that she must do so now and she was given the job of standing in the river and filling huge barrels with a bucket. It was my job to take the barrels to the river in an ox-cart, to collect the water, so I did not get wet. Some of the Russian women working in the river quickly saw this and soon they were screaming at me in Russian.

I knew enough now to understand what they were saying and I swore back at them, until one of them jumped from the river and came towards me. She was screaming that she would kill me. I stood my ground and shouted back. 'Come on,' I said, 'we will see who will be killed.' The woman stopped. I was tall and my shoulders were broad. She turned and went back to the river. No more was I insulted by the Russian women; I would have fought any of them. My whole life was now a fight – to live.

Early one morning in August a large party of us was ordered to help with the harvesting about twenty miles from the village. The work was not hard; huge combine harvesters did most of it, but at the end of the day the lorries did not arrive to take us home. Instead we were led to several large caravans which had been taken to the fields and we were told that we would have to sleep in them, on the hard wooden boards which served as beds. A small field kitchen arrived to give us the first food we had had that day, scraps of mutton and a watery barley soup. It was a horrible meal, but we were hungry and ate it. The night was hot and the caravans were stifling and stuffy, but we dared not sleep outside for fear of the wolves.

The next night was the same; we had to stay in the caravans and for over a week we lived like this until we were filthy. We had no combs to keep our hair tidy and we were allowed no more than a cup of water a day with which to keep ourselves clean, but I quickly learned how to take a mouthful of water, spit it out on my hands and wipe the dust from my face and eyes.

At the end of ten days, when we were taken back to the village, we were alive with fleas, lice and bugs. I was bitten all over and my long hair, although it was plaited and tied with grass, was full of the vermin. It took weeks to get rid of them. When I undid my plaits, they fell out on my dark skirt, hundreds of them. We put paraffin on our hair to try to kill them, but it was a long process and we had to boil our clothes several times before they were clean again. Even then we sat at night searching our clothes, and every day I felt a bite somewhere.

The morning before we ended the harvesting I had risen early and jumped out of the caravan. It was misty and a few miles away I saw what I thought to be a village. I called to the other girls and they saw it too; we thought we had been moved during the night and wondered where we might be. The village was so unlike the other Siberian villages that we had seen, more like a Ukrainian village, with thatched roofs and beautiful green trees. Then, in half an hour, the mist began to clear and we watched as the village disappeared. Our village had been a mirage.

CHAPTER V

The Hunger and the Cold

When the harvesting was over we were started on an even harder job, transporting the grain to the great elevator at Novo Sukhotino. We were told that this job was one of the best paid of the year. It meant ten days almost without a stop and the only sleep we were to get was what we could snatch in our own ox-carts.

Jurek, Kazik, one of his sisters, myself and three Russians from our village were chosen for the job and each of us was given an ox-cart. Then came the race to the farm to get the best oxen; we needed two each, but those who lost the race had the old and thin oxen which could not move so fast or pull such large loads.

I was one of the lucky ones and chose a fine pair of oxen. With shovels we loaded our carts, nearly a ton and a half of beautiful, clean grain to each loading, and then began the journey to the elevator at Novo Sukhotino. At the end of each loading I was almost ready to collapse. All the time we were told to hurry, but as the journey to the elevator took half a day I had plenty of time to regain my strength for the next loading.

As fast as one train was loaded from the elevator another took its place. Much of the food, grain, fats and butter was going to Germany at that time and the Russians were singing a song about it. I cannot remember the words, but the song told of the wonderful things to eat which went west to Germany, and in return the only things which came east were bones and old rags.

When we drew our carts up to the platform beside the elevator, the unloading began without wasting a second. We filled sacks with the grain, hoisted the sacks on our shoulders and carried them up narrow planks to tip them into the elevator. For ten days I did this and at the end my shoulders were almost as strong as a man's. All day and all night the loading and unloading went on; sometimes we would arrive at the elevator at three in the morning and, half asleep, start to fill the sacks at once. On the night journeys with the ox-carts we took it in turns to lead and stay awake so that the others could sleep a little as they went along.

On the third night it was the turn of Kazik to lead and for a long time he kept us awake with his loud songs until eventually I fell into an exhausted sleep. I do not know how long I slept but I was awakened by shouts. It was still dark and my cart was standing alone somewhere out in the fields. Kazik had fallen asleep as he led the carts and the oxen had wandered off to look for grass to eat. Three of the carts were missing when the head of the village came across the tiny convoy; I was the last to be found, far away from the rest, and it was only because my oxen were white that I was eventually seen. Whether or not wolves were near I did not know, but I was frightened as we made our way back to the road and the other carts.

On the fifth day we were told that we were not working fast enough. The oxen were too slow and horses took their place. Then the journeys took half the time, but it meant that we worked twice as hard loading the carts and unloading at the elevator. We were fed at the farm, but the food was not nearly enough for the work, and at the end of the job I was so exhausted that I felt I wanted to die. I slept all through one day and a night.

Now was the time for the villagers to be paid for their labours of the past months. Long queues formed outside the office of the head of the village, but recent arrivals like us were told to wait until the other villagers were dealt with. For two days we watched excitedly as they left the office loaded with sacks of wheat, sacks of potatoes and money. Now it was our turn to line up, but when Jurek and I got to the office my heart sank; we were told there was no more wheat and no more potatoes, as the supply allocated to the village had been exhausted. We demanded our wages in money, but the head man told us this was exhausted too. I cried as we walked away. A winter in Siberia and starvation were staring us in the face. Jurek could say nothing; I think he was near to tears.

That night we made a plan. Day after day we went to the

office asking for our money and day after day we were told there was none for us. The head man told us that if we wanted money we must work for it, but we flatly refused to do any more work. 'If we do not have the same rights as the other villagers in pay,' we told the head man, 'we do not have the same compulsion to work.'

For days we argued and refused to work, but it was hopeless; we had no food and we were getting weak from hunger. We were defeated. Eventually we had to work just to get from the head man the ration tickets which would allow us to buy a little corn from the village store. The other villagers were sorry, but they could not help; their rations had to last a year and they could not sell us food in case they were short later.

The corn we managed to buy we tried to exchange for flour to make bread, but here again we found that it was hopeless. We had to give double the amount of corn for the flour and the flour was coarse, with the chaff still in it.

Time went by and we were getting weaker from hunger. Then one day Jurek took me along and for hours we sat in the office of the head of the village. All the morning he appeared not to notice us, but at last he was forced to speak. We told him we wanted money and he laughed, so we sat in the office until it was closed in the evening.

The next day we did the same and the next day too. The head man was furious, but when he ordered us to go Jurek would always say: 'You cannot throw us out; this is Russia and we all have equal rights.' We continued our squatting tactics for nearly two weeks; from early morning till late at night we refused to move from the office until in desperation the head of the village agreed to pay us.

Even then we found that our efforts had been wasted, Jurek was given a hundred roubles and I was given thirty. I soon found the real value of the wages I had worked so hard for – the price of a loaf of bread was officially half a rouble, but as the winter got harder there was none to be had. The only way to get bread was to buy on the black market – and the price was thirty roubles a loaf.

The Siberian winter was upon us. At first only the nights were cold, but soon the days were cold too. We knew that we would have to save everything we could to get through the winter, and when a railwayman moved from his house into the town the whole of our family moved in together. It was tiny but cheaper; we had one room and it was cold, and we had little fuel to keep it warm.

To wash our clothes and keep the lice from them we had to go to the river. The water was already nearly freezing and soon washing became impossible. Stepmother took charge of the money and eked it out to buy food, and as it got less and less she sold more of our clothes. But the winter was only just beginning; we dared not sell much, for we did not know what we would need in the months that lay ahead.

We bought an ox-calf and when it was killed we sold half to another family. We ate well for a few days, but much of the meat had to be salted and stored for later use. We took the skin to the village, hoping to get a pair of shoes in exchange, but we were told there was enough for one shoe only and we would have to wait until we could get another skin.

One day we were called to the office of the village head to be told that all our possessions in Poland had been sold and we were to receive the money for them. We were handed an official-looking document, typed on beautiful government paper; dozens of articles were listed, but we could see nothing from the big house. The Russians had stolen most of this even before we left and the articles listed were only from the small house into which we had moved. At the bottom of the form was a large sum of money due to us, enough to keep us through the winter, a figure which made me almost cry out with joy. Then Jurek turned over the page and we saw another list: the Russian government had charged the fare for each of us from Poland to Siberia. The food we had on the way was included, and the total just balanced the sum due to us from the sale of what was left behind at the small house, with a few roubles to our credit. The head of the village paid us out and made us sign the receipt.

It was a mockery. My stepmother wept when we got home, but Jurek and I could not cry. We were getting used to this sort of treatment. Our only reaction was disgust.

Now there was little work to do and we spent most of our time queueing at the village shop for such little things as a bar of soap or a small packet of sweets. In November came the first snow; it was terribly cold, but with the snow came another worry.

Jasiek's wife found she was to have another baby. Still weak and ill from the death of little Barbara, she was almost frantic when she realized her condition. We tried to comfort her; we told her that it was the best thing to have another baby now that Barbara was gone, but we all dreaded the time when she was due to have it. We knew that Barbara's birth had been difficult and had nearly killed them both.

The neighbours were kind when they heard the news; none of them could afford much but they sent Jasiek's wife little things to eat. The rest of us in the house went without food many times so that she could have enough; she had to be strong to survive her next ordeal.

Our meals were becoming more and more frugal. For breakfast we had soup made from two potatoes and two peppers; with a piece of bread each this had to suffice for the whole family, but the bread was like clay and almost uneatable unless it was dipped in the soup. The villagers had been given so little this year that the only corn they sold was three or four years old, hard, rough and sour.

The only other meal of the day was almost the same, except that sometimes we could add scraps of meat to the soup. It was as well that there was no work to be done; we were not strong enough to do much else than sit in the house all day.

Soon this became unbearable. We were so short of fuel that we could not even get the dried manure to keep the stove going. We went for several days without cooked food until Jurek managed to find some dried grass to burn, but this gave out such bitter and choking fumes that we were all coughing from morning until night. Even the bread tasted of the bitter, dried grass and we could not eat it. We had to find some other fuel.

Jurek had an idea: trains from Karaganda, the mining town some hundreds of miles to the south, passed Novo Sukhotino every half an hour or so. Huge modern engines pulled the trains along the single line and when another train wished to pass one of them would pull into a siding.

At first we walked along the side of the line picking up pieces of coal which had dropped from the trucks. But often we would spend all day and bring home hardly enough to keep the stove going for more than an hour. So Jurek carried his idea further. He had watched the loaded trains pull into the sidings and worked out the approximate times. Then he brought several of his friends into the plan and when a train stopped on the siding Jurek jumped on to one of the wagons. He tied a rope to the pin which held the doors closed, and when the train passed a prearranged spot, as near to our village as possible, Jurek pulled the rope and out came the pin.

Almost a whole truck-load of coal fell beside the line. Jurek jumped off the train at the next stop and made his way back whilst we filled sacks with the coal and carried them to the village. Nearly the whole of the village turned out to grab the coal as it fell from the trains, but it was not long before the Russian officials discovered what had happened. Eventually a Russian commissar arrived. He accused us of sabotage and threatened horrible penalties if anyone was caught. But he could prove nothing and we stole many wagon-loads of coal before it became too dangerous to carry on.

To occupy ourselves we went to the village every morning to wait for the post. Nothing ever seemed to come for us, but it was something to do and we often heard scraps of news from those who did receive letters. One morning it was my turn to wait for the post and I noticed the snow beginning to blow along the street, the top layer wriggling along like a mass of snakes. Then a wind sprang up.

The sky was still clear, but quickly the wind got stronger. It was whistling in an eerie way and the villagers told me to hurry home; a blizzard was on the way, they said, but the postman had not arrived and I decided to wait another few minutes.

In that time the sky became black and I started to make for home, but in seconds the blizzard had come. It beat into my face, stinging and scratching until I pulled a scarf across and up to my eyes. It beat into my eyes until I was forced to pull the scarf higher to cover them. I staggered blindly through the street, hoping I was going in the right direction, until at last someone grabbed my arm and I heard the muffled voice of a boy who lived near us. Together we made our way home, but by then I was exhausted and bruised all over from the buffeting of the storm.

For the rest of the day we could not leave the house, and in the evening, when we needed water, Jurek tied himself to a rope and we all held on to it as he made his way to the well. In just those few yards he might have been lost if we had not been able to pull him back.

For three days and nights the blizzard raged, keeping us in the house, and after the second day our small store of food was gone. We prayed that the blizzard would stop; we had no fuel, it was bitter and we thought that we must soon freeze to death. When we slept we put on every piece of clothing we could find. We huddled close together, but nothing, it seemed, could keep us warm.

On the third morning I woke early; the noise of the blizzard had stopped and I could hear the sounds of people outside. I lit the paraffin lamp but could see nothing through the windows; a thick layer of ice covered them on the inside and beyond was blackness.

I went to the tiny door and opened it inwards, but a solid mass of snow shut out the light. It took us over an hour to dig our way through it until we saw the sun and a clear sky. Huge drifts of snow were banked up all around us; only five inches of our walls were showing above the snow. If the blizzard had continued for another few days it would have buried us completely.

Now we were well into December, but for some time we had no more heavy snow. Sometimes I visited my mother-in-law, usually when Kazik was not there, but one day he was sitting by the fire when I arrived. I had not seen him for several weeks and he tried to kiss me. I turned away from him quickly, but his arms were around me and he was asking me to return to him. I was sorry then that I had gone to the house. I ran home like a frightened child.

Daily we waited in the village for the post until one day, shortly before Christmas, the head of the village handed Jurek a letter addressed to my stepmother. Quickly we looked at it; it bore a Polish stamp, but with the head of Hitler.

Jurek clasped my hand and I felt my heart beginning to

pound. I wanted to cry out, but neither of us could utter a word. We had recognized the handwriting – it was my father's. We wanted to tear the letter open but it was not addressed to us, so we started to run and did not stop until we reached the house, shouting for our stepmother yards before we got to the door.

She took the letter and her hands shook as she opened it; then she began to read, words written by the father we had not seen for all these months, not knowing whether he was alive or dead.

His story unfolded slowly as my stepmother read a few words and paused to smother her sobs. Father had been in the Russian jail at Kharkov when he had heard of the German request for repatriation of all the German, Austrian and Czecho-Slovakian nationals who were being held by the Russians. Several men from the jail had been repatriated and father had tried to join them by saying that he was German. 'I went on hunger strike for days until I was in a coma,' he wrote. 'Finally they believed my story and I was sent here to German-occupied Poland.'

Father, of course, was not German, but his name – Laessig – was; he spoke the language well and part of his family had come from Germany. He seemed to apologize for what he had done but explained: 'In Russia there was no hope for me at all. It was just a matter of time before I died in jail like so many of the others, and I know you will understand why I took this step. From here I can see the only chance of getting you all out of Siberia.'

Father, the letter went on, was living in Warsaw with his two married sisters, helping them to run a café. Both the sisters were married to Polish officers and one of these had escaped through Sweden to join the Polish army in England, I later found out. The Germans knew nothing of this and when my aunts were questioned by them they simply replied: 'We do not know where our husbands are. We think they were taken by the Russians.'

The aunt who had tried to persuade Jurek and me to go with her to Germany from Rovno had been a great help in securing my father's release. Relations of hers in Germany were in the diplomatic service and they had arranged for a strong recommendation to be sent to the Russians. The letter came to an end with these words: 'I am trying to do everything possible for you, but I must impress on you that if anyone asks what you are, you must insist that you are German.'

My stepmother put down the letter and we all began to talk at once. Jurek, who had always refused to say that he was German when we had the chance, so long before, to escape from Russian-occupied Poland, was almost dancing for joy. 'What does it matter now if we say we are German,' he was saying. 'So long as we are with papa, it doesn't matter what we say.'

We should have been happy that day, but our gaiety lasted for seconds only. My stepmother spoke. 'Never, never will I say that I am German,' she declared; 'I would rather stay and die in Siberia.'

We were dumbfounded; we began arguing at once, but my stepmother quickly silenced me. I was married to Wasilewski, she said, and had no right to go at all. But Jurek could do as he pleased. Little more was said but my mind was made up. If I had the chance, I would swear I was German – anything to get away from Siberia, its squalor, starvation and misery.

From then on Jurek and I felt that we had something to live for; letters from father came almost regularly, once a fortnight, and the neighbours crowded into our house to hear the news. In one letter father said that living conditions in German-occupied Poland were little better than in the eastern sector. He did not try to excuse the Germans for starting the war, but said: 'At least it is possible to deal with the Germans; either by tears or money we can get things done. With the Russians it does not matter what you do; they are impossible to deal with.'

We gathered that father and his sisters could live only by dealing on the black market in the drinks which they were allocated for the café. Father hated it, he said, but explained that it was the only way; everybody was living in the same way. And father had to have the food to build himself up; he was weak and half-starved from his stay in Russian jails.

About Christmas time the word 'escape' was mentioned for the first time. Jurek and I were alone. He was already impatient and said, 'I must get to papa. Even if I escape from here, I must do so soon.'

At once I pleaded to go with him. I had not thought of

escaping since that day we gathered water from beside the railway line on our journey to Siberia and had no idea how it could be done. But I pleaded not to be left behind. Jurek sat silently for a moment and then he spoke. 'No, Eugenia,' he said, 'if I go I must go alone. If you were with me and something happened to us, father would never forgive me.'

I knew it was no use; Jurek had made up his mind, but we were hoping that our release might come through official channels. It was a long time before I heard the word 'escape' again.

Christmas in Siberia was for our family a bleak affair. Not a tiny extra thing to eat could we get. On Christmas Eve hardly a word passed between us as we sat over the thin potato soup and small piece of the hard, clay-like bread. Still hungry, I was about to go to bed to keep warm when Kazik's sister Christina arrived to ask if we would all go to her mother's house for the evening. But Jasiek's wife was ill and, because of this, all the others politely refused the invitation.

Except me. I longed for the excuse to leave the dark and dreary house, so with Christina I hurried down the street and into the comparative cheerfulness of the other house. Many people were there, friends and neighbours. I saw Kazik, but he hardly spoke as I arrived. The room was bright with candles and Kazik's mother had made a brave attempt to keep the Polish custom of providing twelve dishes for the Christmas Eve celebration. It must have been so difficult for her; nothing was plentiful, but she had saved the food for weeks for this night.

Our custom was never to eat meat on this night, but without it we could not have had this meal. To me it tasted wonderful and I had the best meal in weeks. Kazik's mother pressed the food on me; she knew how much I needed it and later, when Kazik asked me again to return to him, his mother did not try to dissuade me.

She put her arms around me as though I were her own daughter. 'Why don't you come to live with us?' she asked. 'You need looking after; you are so thin and weak. If you come here I can feed you and I will find you a bed all to yourself near the oven.'

I wanted to say yes; the house and the food I needed so much, but I could not bring myself to live with Kazik. I thanked his mother and promised that I would think it over, then I went back to our house, to the dim light of the single paraffin lamp and the gloomy faces as they ate their second meal of the day – more potato soup, more hard, clay-like bread.

On Christmas Day I did not leave the house. Our food was barely enough to keep body and soul together. We were short of fuel and we went to bed early. It was warmer than sitting around the bare and sordid room. I cried myself to sleep that night.

Early in January my stepmother was called to the village. A commissar had arrived to question her. 'What is your name?' he asked and she answered, 'Laessig.'

'Are you German?'

'No, I am Polish.'

'Is your husband German?'

'I suppose so. He is in Germany.'

'He makes a request for three children. Who is Jurek?'

'He is my stepson.'

'What was his mother?'

'Half Polish, half Russian.'

'Eugenia, what is she?'

'The same as Jurek, they are brother and sister.'

'Henryk?'

'He is my son and I am Polish.'

The Commissar wrote down the answer to each question and my stepmother said: 'We would all like to go to my husband. We were promised that we would be with him, but the promise has not been kept.'

The commissar did not reply. He closed the book. 'That is all. You may go,' was all he said.

When she got home my stepmother told us of the questions. 'I could not lie,' she said. 'They knew I was not German.' She would not talk of the interview again, but Jurek and I knew of the terrible struggle which was going on in her mind. If she had lied we might have been able to join father. But she would have had to leave her parents and Jasiek and his wife behind in Siberia.

It was some time before we heard of the Russian answer to my father's request: 'We are sorry, there are no Germans in Siberja.'

January dragged on, conditions got no better and many people fell ill from starvation. There was work to do but few of us were strong enough, and even if we had worked we knew there would be no pay. Once we heard that there was still wheat beneath the snow at a spot out on the steppes and Jurek worked for two days to get permission to use an ox-cart to find it. All day he dug through the frozen snow until, at last, he found the wheat. There was little to be had, but every grain was precious.

Soon we were completely without fuel and it was then Jurek taught me to steal. I did not know until then that he had been stealing for weeks, and whether I liked it or not I had to steal too. I had to become a thief to live.

We would not steal from our neighbours, but Jurek knew that up at the farm there were stacks of the dried manure we needed so much as fuel. One night Jurek worked out his plan and he, Jasiek and I set out with large sacks. It was midnight; the moon was bright and the snow creaked under our feet as we walked the two miles to the stacks. I was sure someone would shoot at us, but that night we were lucky.

We reached the stacks of manure and began to fill our sacks. When mine was full I tried to lift it. I heaved and heaved at the sack which a few months before I would have lifted with ease, but it would not budge. I was too weak and I almost cried with frustration as I took some of the manure out again. For the second time I tried to lift it, but again it was too much for me.

In the end the sack was only a third full and I got it on my back only with the help of Jasiek and Jurek. For the two miles back home I staggered under the load, forgetting that we might be shot at any moment. I was too upset at finding I was not strong enough to carry as much as Jasiek and Jurek.

Jurek did not want me to go again; he told me that the load I carried was not worth the danger of being caught. But I had to go, for every piece of manure I could steal meant we could stay warm for a little longer. But the trips to the farm did not last long; someone realized that the manure was disappearing and

one night we saw the dark outline of a guard with a fixed
bayonet as we approached the stacks. Silently we turned and
crawled on our stomachs until we were well away. Then we ran.
We dared not chance it again.

Soon Jurek found something else to steal; it was coal again,
but we had to wait until it was snowing before we made our way
to the house of the foreman who lived on the nearest farm. Only
then were we sure that no one would be around and we found
our way there by following the telephone lines.

Several times we made the journey. At the back of the foreman's house we found the coal store. We filled our sacks and
stole away through the snowstorm. Then one day I did not go
with Jurek and he was nearly caught. He had just filled a sack
and was making his way along the road. It was snowing hard
and suddenly Jurek came face to face with the foreman.
Nothing was said and Jurek hurried on his way, scared that the
man was after him.

The following day the foreman came to our house. We knew
at once why he had come and we expected the worst. Not a word
was said by Jurek, Jasiek or myself, and it was my stepmother
who spoke to the visitor. We waited for him to say something
about the coal, but instead he stood and looked around the bare,
dark room. Irena, Jasiek's wife, was lying in a corner, ill and
weak, and my stepbrother was crying for food, he was so
hungry. The foreman turned to the door and called Jurek
outside. 'If you steal coal be careful not to meet me again,' he
said. 'I know you are freezing, but if you fall into my hands you
know what I must do.'

He said no more, but went away. We did not go to his house
again.

One morning Jurek woke me early. 'I have something to tell
you,' he whispered, 'but I am afraid to tell stepmother. You
know how worried she is about getting into trouble.' Jasiek's
wife Irena awoke and Jurek told us both what he had done.

'I have stolen twelve chickens,' he told us. 'They are all dead.
I've wrung their necks. But I was afraid to bring them into
the house. They are in a sack and buried in the snow in the
garden.'

To Irena and me the news was wonderful. There was almost

nothing else to eat in the house and Irena said: 'Don't worry, Jurek. We are going to eat those chickens whatever your stepmother says.'

All that day we were busy plucking the chickens, but we were careful that not one feather went astray. We put them in a sack and buried it as deep in the snow as we could dig. Jurek ate a whole chicken that evening and we knew that he deserved it; we cooked the others one a day and shared each between us. We even crunched the bones to suck every bit of goodness out of them and where the bones were soft we ate those too. There was almost nothing left to burn; we had not eaten so well for so long.

It was as well that we were careful to burn even tiny pieces of bone, for, a few days after we ate our first chicken, two Russian commissars suddenly appeared at the house. Without asking, they pushed their way in and searched every corner. Two pigs had been stolen from the farm, they said, and they questioned us all before they were satisfied and left.

For two days they searched the houses but they found nothing. Three Polish boys from the other end of the village had stolen the pigs, we were secretly told, and they had been cut up quickly and shared among as many people as possible. Every morsel had been eaten before the commissars discovered what had happened and, although the three boys were questioned, they were not suspected.

We thought that the inquiries would stop then but the commissars stayed in the village; for days they continued their inquiries and finally arrested two Russian men. We knew that they had nothing to do with the theft of the pigs but the commissars, it seemed, were determined that someone should be blamed. For three days they held the two Russians until they signed confessions; the men were then taken away and we did not see them again.

We waited until everything had quietened down before Jurek discovered something else to steal. Up at the farm huge loads of timber had been delivered to build a new barn. They had been there for weeks. So we set out on our pillaging expeditions once more, but we chose the nights when it was snowing and dark. A dozen times we stole home in the early hours, each carrying a five-foot length of the timber, until Jurek decided that if we stole any more it would surely be noticed.

It seemed that there was nothing else we could steal, but Jurek was still not lost for ideas. Night after night he would go out to houses in the village with his concertina and sing and play to the villagers. He wished to be paid, he told the villagers, but not with money. They offered him lots of drink, but this he refused; he insisted on being paid with food. And night after night Jurek brought something home for us, mostly scraps. Jurek saved us from complete starvation.

Eventually, if Jurek found something to steal I could not go with him, because I was so thin and weak that when I tried to walk to the village centre I had to stop several times to rest. It was our custom that anyone could visit a house to rest and if there was something warm to drink he was given it. At many of the houses at which I was forced to stop I did not know the people; but it made no difference, I would rest for half an hour or so, take anything that was offered me and leave.

The winter got colder and hunger grew worse. An old man and a child, too weak to survive, died and in almost every house someone in the family lay ill and at death's door. And then one night we heard the dreaded sound of wolves. They were as hungry as we were, killing any animal they could find. Even dogs disappeared and were never seen again. For days and days we were terrified to go out after dusk; we just sat and listened to the distant sound of the wolves and prayed that they would not come near the house.

Once when Jurek was up in the fields collecting grass to burn, a deer rushed towards him. Jurek at first thought that he was being attacked, but the deer stopped and stood beside him, quivering. Then Jurek heard the sound of the wolves; soon he could see them a few hundred yards away. They stopped when they saw Jurek and the deer stayed close to him in terror. For nearly an hour they stood like this but, seeing a man, the wolves did not attack. Eventually they went away, but the deer followed Jurek closely for a long time as he made his way back to the village.

Jurek told us what had happened. 'I should have killed the deer,' he said. 'It would have been meat for us for many days.

But I could not kill it; I was too sorry for the poor beast. It seemed just like us, hunted all the time and so afraid. It was like a little child.'

Things could get no worse, it seemed, but even now Siberia had not tortured us enough. Money was getting so short that we had to leave our house and move into one with a young Russian couple and their baby; we were now in a room even smaller than the one we had had before. When it was burning, the stove in the other room, where the Russian family lived, slightly warmed one wall of ours. We had no boards to make a bed and at night we huddled as close to the wall as possible.

CHAPTER VI

Planning to Escape

At the beginning of February Jasiek's wife Irena had her baby. Early one morning she began screaming with pain and my stepbrother was quickly put in the kitchen with the Russian family. For eight hours we sat there whilst the baby was being born and Irena moaned and screamed. Jasiek and my stepmother's mother did all they could, though it seemed an age to me before they delivered the baby. We thought that all was over, but then complications set in and Irena was screaming again.

Jasiek rushed to the village for help, but there was none to be had. He was almost demented, but finally he managed to get a horse and sledge from the farm and drove to Novo Sukhotino to bring back a woman doctor. He was away for hours and we thought Irena must die before the doctor arrived.

The doctor was annoyed at being called; she complained that there was nothing to worry about, but it was a long time before she left, sure that Irena would be safe. I sat petrified throughout the day; I knew how calves and pigs were born, but this was my first experience of human birth. The screams frightened me; I tried not to look, but I could not close my ears to Irena's pain. Jurek vomited for hours; he could not stand it.

When the danger had passed the tension broke. Jasiek, who looked like a ghost, swore that he would never allow his wife to go through such agony again. The baby survived, a boy, very big, and they called him Bohdan. But Jasiek had to work for a week on the farm, carrying grass and fodder for the animals, to pay for the loan of the horse and sledge.

With the birth of the new baby the cramped conditions in the room became unbearable. From somewhere hordes of fleas and lice attacked us incessantly and night after night we worked through the seams of our clothes, picking out the lice and dropping them into a small bottle. The lice from my clothes were easy to catch; I was so weak that I was sure they were not feeding well! My stepmother's father was ill with influenza and for some reason the lice did not attack him at all.

We were barely existing. From morning till night we froze and sometimes for days on end we had nothing at all to eat. Gradually I became aware that my stepmother and her family resented the fact that I was in the house with them. One day in February, after we had not eaten for two days, it became too much for her. 'You are married,' she said. 'You should be with your husband. You are not our responsibility now. We have not enough even for ourselves.'

I burst into tears. I staggered to my mother-in-law to tell her what had happened and collapsed when I reached the house; for weeks I had had nothing to eat except scraps of bread.

Kazik's mother did everything she could. She gave me a little cheese she had made, but my stomach was so shrunken that at first I could not eat. She begged me to stay and told me that I need not stay as a wife to her son. I did not know what else to do, where else to go. I agreed.

The family tried to make me comfortable, but even here the conditions were cramped and all of us except my mother-in-law and her husband had to sleep in one huge bed. True, I had more to eat than I had had with my own family, but it was very little more. It was almost impossible to buy food anywhere now. Anyone who had some was jealously guarding it, for they did not know where the next would come from. I was now so weak and depressed that I could not even pray; indeed, there seemed nothing left to pray for. And the news which filtered through from Poland made me sure that the end could come only in death. Germany was winning the war, we were told; she had taken Greece and Norway. Help for us at that time seemed a million years away.

But gradually my unhappiness taught me to pray again, to ask God to let me die. Night after night I stole out of the house and knelt in the snow. To kill myself was against my religion and for that I knew I could never be forgiven. But I thought that if

I helped God as I prayed to him, he would help me to die from the freezing coldness of the night air.

At first I stayed in the snow for as long as half an hour, holding my Madonna to me as I prayed, but soon I was missed from the house. Night after night they found me and carried me back; my mother-in-law tried to comfort me, but I waited impatiently for the next night so that I could kneel in the snow again, praying for God's help to die.

Kazik said little; we spoke to each other only when we had to. He could not understand me and did not seem to be annoyed, but often he said, 'You are crazy, you do not know what you want.'

The atmosphere in the house was always tense when Kazik was there. He argued with his father when he held our weekly religious service; he sat on a chair while we all knelt. Kazik refused to kneel; if his father could sit, Kazik argued, then he would sit too. For his younger brother Witold, Kazik had nothing but hatred; for a long time I wondered why and then one day his sister Christina told me the reason.

I had known Witold as a friend of my brother and he often visited us in our early days in Siberia. Then, when I became engaged to Kazik, he suddenly stopped coming. Witold had wanted to marry me, Christina said, but Kazik had insisted that as the older brother he should marry me. He had forbidden Witold to visit us when we became engaged and had disliked Witold ever since. Never once did Witold show his feelings, but I was even more unhappy when I learned the truth. I felt that I could not stay in the house when Witold and Kazik were together and began to visit Gunia, almost daily.

Gunia was always sympathetic, she seemed to understand and I felt better after talking to her. 'You must not worry,' she told me. 'You are young and have no children. It is so much more difficult for Irena; she has a baby to feed and bring up.'

One night I was sitting with Gunia when we heard a bell ringing in the street outside; a Russian soldier was calling everyone to the club. I felt weak, but Gunia held my arm as we made our way there. It was warmer inside and I was glad that I had agreed to go. But I was not glad when I heard the speech made by the political commissar who had come to the village for that evening. He stood in front of a large map of Europe and Russia and explained how the war was progressing. 'Germany is winning the war against England,' he said, 'and soon that war will be over. But now is the time for Russia to build up her strength, her stockpiles of food and arms. For Germany will be weak when she has won the war and she will not have the population to occupy all she has won.'

The commissar's eyes were alight as he went on and there were gasps from many of us as he said: 'Germany is winning this part of the war for us; when it is finished we must then vanquish Germany. We must be strong, for we will have the world at our feet.'

I felt shocked as we made our way back to Gunia's house and the full realization of our own position gradually came to my mind: we were doomed to stay in Siberia now to help the Russian war effort. But more than that the commissar had pointed out our complete helplessness. He had told us the Russian plans, knowing that from Siberia we could do absolutely nothing about them.

That evening I had seen Kazik at the club; he was sitting at the front with his arm around a young Russian teacher and did not see me until we were leaving. He loved to try to make me jealous, but he was surprised when he realized that I had been watching him. It meant nothing to me; I had no feelings for him and my mind was too full of what I had heard. I was miserable and only wanted to get away from the club.

Back at Kazik's house that night there was a terrible argument; both his sisters had been at the club and they had told their mother of Kazik being with the Russian teacher. As soon as I entered I found myself involved in the argument, but I could take no more. That night I told my stepmother that I must leave the house, and the following day I returned to my stepmother and the tiny, cramped hovel in which my family was living.

Now it was the end of March; the weather was not quite so cold, but it still snowed occasionally. I tried again to help Jurek when he went to find food or fuel but I still had little strength and could walk for short distances only.

I had been back with the family for only a week or so when

I felt I was becoming weaker, a strange weakness I had not felt before. I wanted to do nothing but lie in the room all day. Then a dreadful feeling of sickness came over me. I was ill, I was sure; starvation and the cold of Siberia were claiming me. I did not want to fight. At last my prayers were being answered; I was about to die.

But death never came and after two weeks, when I seemed to get no worse, I told my stepmother. She listened quietly as I explained, then she calmly answered: 'Eugenia, you are going to have a baby. There is nothing to be done.'

What was she saying? I sat in a daze, unable to think. Then with a rush, it flooded into my brain. I cried out, I screamed, 'Oh no, no!' and ran from the house. Through the snow I half ran, half stumbled. My mind was in a whirl, but all the time in the background the words were beating a tattoo, 'You're going to have a baby.' I reached my mother-in-law's house and fell crying to the floor.

Only mother-in-law, Christina and Czesia were there and minutes passed before they could quieten me. I sobbed out what my stepmother had told me and they implored me not to worry. It might not be so, they said; but as I explained the symptoms my mother-in-law shook her head. 'It is so, Eugenia,' she said, as she put her arms around me. 'You are going to have a baby, but it is nothing to be afraid of. We must look after you and make you fit.'

I begged them not to tell Kazik, and they gave me their promise. They would not let me leave until I had stopped crying and they gave me a little food. Still in a daze I walked home and went straight to bed.

But sleep was impossible. Hour after hour the thoughts went through my mind. First I thought of Irena when she had her baby and I was sure I would die when my time came. Then I made up my mind to kill myself and thought of ways of doing it, but broke into sobs when I told myself how wicked that would be.

I thought with horror of bringing a child into such a world as Siberia, with its poverty, its starvation, of years and years of working on farms, of years and years of near-death as each winter came and went. I could not bear the thoughts which chased each other round and round my head. I felt it would burst.

Now dawn was breaking and my head was clearing; like the new day outside it was as if the darkness had suddenly been taken from my mind. It came to me at once: I would escape. No child of mine would be born in a captivity such as ours. I did not think of how it could be done; only the one word sang in my head – escape.

From that moment I changed. The tiredness seemed to leave me as if by magic. The sickness came again that morning, but I hardly noticed it. I had to tell someone what was on my mind; I was sure that otherwise my head would burst.

But who? Jurek? No, he would never agree to help me, he had already told me that if anything happened to me he would feel responsible. My stepmother? No, she would do everything she could to stop me in case there was trouble for us all. My mother-in-law? No again, Kazik would hear of it and I felt sure he would stop me.

There was only one person I could talk to, so early that morning I hurried to the house where Gunia lived. I knew she would do anything to help me; she would not try to stop me. I knew I could rely on Gunia, but I was not prepared for what she said after I told her of my plan.

She listened quietly as I told her that I was going to have a baby. She did not say a word when I told her that I had planned to commit suicide. From my face she must have guessed what was on my mind, and when I finished with the words, 'I have made up my mind to escape,' she smiled. I saw her eyes shining. She took many seconds to reply, then she said, 'Eugenia, if you go I shall go with you. We must escape; that is the only way for us both.'

All that morning we discussed it. We would have to start right away selling our clothes to get money for the journey. We must buy Russian clothes as a disguise and we decided to time our escape for May 1st, a Russian public holiday and not far away. Everything we could think of we discussed. But how we were to get out of Siberia neither of us knew. In any case, at that time it did not seem important.

Now I had something to live for. I was weak but I was filled

F

with a new zest. A week before I could not have attempted the journey, but the following day I set off for Novo Sukhotino with a small bundle of clothes. I took two of the best dresses I had and some underclothes; I sold them easily and two days later prepared another bundle. I left the house quietly and made for the road to Novo Sukhotino. Someone was running behind me. I stopped and turned, Jurek was following me.

He had guessed, I knew. I expected an argument, but instead Jurek was saying, 'Wait for me, I am coming with you.' He, too, carried a small bundle and fell in step beside me. 'You are planning to escape; I know it,' he said, 'but I will not stop you. I am planning to escape, too, but we must not go together. You may go before or after me, it does not matter. But I cannot take you with me.'

Jurek was hoping to leave soon, he told me, the snow was melting fast and the floods were sweeping down on many of the low-lying Siberian villages. Thousands of people would be evacuating from the floods, Jurek said; the railways would be packed and he thought this the best time to make his bid.

I told him of my plan to leave on May 1st and Jurek thought it excellent; the weather would be better then, he said, and I thought that he would postpone his attempt until about the same time. He would not discuss how he was going to leave and did not ask me my plan. But he insisted that we keep complete secrecy at home. 'Not a soul must know,' said Jurek: 'We must never discuss this again.'

That day Jurek sold his boots in the town. They were well worn, but he got a good price for them. Now he was left with only a very old and worn pair of shoes. I sold all the clothes I had taken and we went back home that night well satisfied; my store of escape money was growing fast. Gradually I sold almost every piece of spare clothing I had, dresses, light shoes, nightdresses which I had never had the chance to wear, and even some children's clothes which I had kept in my baggage. One dress I had worn when I was seven years old; it was pink, embroidered with daisies and thrilled the woman to whom I sold it.

Then I heard that a troupe of actresses had arrived at Novo Sukhotino and were staying for a week. With my best summer dresses, which I had kept till the last, I hurried to the town once again. The actresses thought the dresses were wonderful and paid from thirty to fifty roubles for each of them. By now I had amassed over three hundred roubles and my stepmother knew that I was selling. But she did not realize to what extent and so far she was not asking me for the money. She must have thought that I would give it to her later, for at that time I do not believe she thought I was planning to escape.

The next part of my plan was to buy Russian clothes; I knew that I must not wear a thing which might give me away. So Gunia and I went on the shopping expedition together. The first essential was a strong pair of boots, I did not know how long they would have to last and they would have to be the best that I could buy. They proved most difficult to find, for there was nothing to be had in my small size and eventually I had to make do with a pair of men's sports boots, laced up around the ankles and with thick rubber soles. They must have been at least two inches too long, but I found that if I laced them tightly and padded the toes with cotton wool they were fairly comfortable. I knew that the odd size would not look suspicious, for the Russians wore such a motley collection of boots, shoes and foot coverings that I would appear lucky to have any type of boot at all.

I bought a black skirt, buttoned at the back and quite modern in Russia at that time, then a white and pink striped blouse, buttoned at the front and with cuffs like a man's shirt. The only stockings I could find were brown and made of heavy, rough cotton, so badly worn that they had hardly any feet left. But they had to do. Woollen pullovers or cardigans were unobtainable in Siberia. But because the weather was still cold I bought a black velvet maternity-style jacket to wear over the blouse. Over that I planned to wear the fur jacket I had been given by the dentist's wife, and I finished my disguise by buying two head-scarves to wear in the Russian fashion. The one which went across my forehead was white, the other over my head and down my face was in brown check. I practised how to tie it, twisted under the chin, round the neck and knotted at the back. I felt sure then that I could pass as a Russian anywhere.

My jewellery I found impossible to sell; it was worthless in Siberia. Gold was of use only to a dentist, but there was no dentist in Novo Sukhotino and the rest of the jewellery was regarded simply as metal and coloured stones. But I kept it still in the tiny bag which hung around my neck. There was little else I would take with me, but I remembered the silver Madonna. I had never been parted from it and I decided to tie it between my two identity cards and hang them around my neck too.

One of my identity cards was in the name of Laessig; it had been issued to me at Aleksandriya. The other was in my married name of Wasilewska. Both bore photographs of me and my fingerprints, and were bound in stiff, black covers with the hammer and sickle insignia. The one in the name of Wasilewska bore the name of the town Novo Sukhotino, and it would have been known immediately that I had escaped from that area if I ever had to produce it in another part of Russia. I was hoping that the one in the name of Laessig would be a help later.

Jurek, I noticed, was getting his escape clothes together quickly. He bought a Russian jacket and a pair of Russian army trousers, thick and quilted, but he could not buy shoes or boots. He had hoped to get new soles for the only pair of shoes he had left, but this proved impossible. They were full of holes and I knew that they would not last more than a day or so on the road.

On the evening of April 12th I arranged to go to the club; there was dancing that night and my escape decision had given me new strength to enjoy it. I dressed in my Russian skirt and blouse and the sports boots with their cotton wool padding, and I was about to leave the house when Jurek called to me. 'Would you lend me your boots?' he asked. 'I want to go out, but my shoes are too bad to wear.'

I needed the boots. I was going dancing, I said, but Jurek laughed. 'They are too big for you,' he chided. 'Anyway you will never be able to dance in them. They have rubber soles. You can find some others to wear. Lend me the boots.'

Reluctantly I took off the boots and gave them to Jurek; they fitted him well and he told me that I had bought well. But I had to borrow shoes from my stepmother before I could go to the club.

I had not been there long when I noticed Jurek standing on a bench, looking at a large map of Russia which hung on the wall. Other young people were making fun of him. 'Look at Jurek,' they were saying. 'He is seeing how the war is going and working out when we shall be liberated.' Jurek did not hear. For a full half-hour he studied the map; the music and dancing went on around him, but he did not appear to notice.

And me? I was happy, my mind was made up and I had a plan. So it was that when a Russian boy, a member of the Communist Youth Movement, came to me and stamped his feet I agreed to dance. For over an hour he did this, continually coming for each dance and stamping his feet in front of me, and each dance I accepted until finally I turned away to another boy, stamped my feet in front of him and danced gaily away.

At the end of the dance friends pulled me to the side of the hall. 'Do you know what you have done?' they asked and their faces were worried. 'You accepted the love dance with the Russian boy. He was proposing to you. Then you insulted him by turning away and dancing with someone else.'

I had not realized this. It was a Russian dance I had not seen before and it had been fun. 'Don't be silly,' I told my friends. 'I cannot marry the boy. I am already married to Kazik.'

My friends were still worried. 'That means nothing,' they told me. 'You have only to pay five roubles and you are married to the Russian boy. You must explain to him. You must apologize.'

I did, but I felt stupid as I explained. The Russian boy appeared to understand, but I could see that he was upset. It seemed that he had really thought I would marry him.

It was nearly midnight when we left the club and the snow was thawing fast. The top was still frozen but underneath it was turning to water. Some of the people sank in the snow almost to their waists when they tried to walk on it, so we all decided to roll over the top down the two hundred yards or so from the club to the main street. Amid laughter many fell through the top layer and were drenched. But tonight for some reason it was fun. We were all in high spirits and I made my way home.

My stepmother opened the door when I arrived and instantly I saw that Jurek was not there. I asked where he was, but stepmother replied: 'He went out about an hour ago, and I don't know where he went. He will come home late again, I expect.'

To her it seemed normal and she added: 'Or he will stay out all night and come home some time tomorrow, as he often does.'

For a long time that night I could not sleep, but Jurek did not return. The next day, April 13th, was exactly a year from the day when we had been taken from Poland and the significance kept me awake. Even now I could hardly believe the thought that would not leave me; I still felt sure that Jurek would turn up before the evening.

It was six o'clock the next evening when I heard someone at the door. I ran there praying it was Jurek, but instead a Russian boy of about fifteen was waiting for me. 'Are you Eugenia, Jurek's sister?' he asked. I nodded and he thrust a small piece of paper in my hand and walked away.

Quickly I unfolded the paper. There on one side was a short message written in Polish so that the Russian boy could not understand it. 'I am going away and have taken your boots,' it said, 'but I have left my fur coat with a man in the village whose address is written here. He will give you money for the coat or you may have the coat itself.'

My heart was beating furiously as I read the note. Jurek had gone. But now it had happened I did not know whether to feel frightened or thrilled. I turned the note over, saw there the name and address of a man in the village, and quickly pushed it out of sight into my pocket.

I was full of dread that my stepmother would ask about the caller, but she said nothing when I went back into the house. When later in the evening she mentioned Jurek I dared not answer. When I went to bed I stood my silver Madonna in its case beside me and prayed for Jurek's safety and success. And I prayed for my own success when the time came for me to follow him. I did not know as I prayed that I would never see Jurek again.

The next morning I went to the man who had Jurek's fur coat and he gave me two hundred roubles. I knew that he would have given Jurek much more and when I complained the man silenced me quickly. 'Your brother has escaped,' he said quickly. 'Many people in the village are talking about it. Take the money and say nothing. I want no trouble.'

The news had travelled quickly. Someone had seen Jurek at

the railway station at Novo Sukhotino early the previous morning. He had been inquiring about the times of trains and there was only one reason for this, everyone knew. I hurried to Gunia with the news and told her that we, too, must go quickly, but Gunia did not agree. 'We must wait until Jurek's escape has quietened down,' she said. 'We will go on May 1st, as we planned.'

I had to agree. Trouble was bound to come now that it was known that Jurek had gone. Still I did not breathe a word of what I knew when I got home.

Five days later my stepmother was called to the village. A furious political commissar had arrived. 'Your son Jurek has escaped,' he shouted at my stepmother. 'You are responsible. Why did you let him go?' Stepmother protested that she could not be responsible. 'Jurek is twenty-one,' she said, but the commissar shouted at her: 'You knew of the escape,' he stormed, 'and it was your duty to report to us. You must not leave the village. If your son is caught he will be punished and you will be punished with him.'

Stepmother tried to explain that she knew nothing of Jurek's escape but it made no difference. 'It is your duty to the state to report anyone you know is planning to escape,' she was told. 'If you know, you are just as guilty as they.'

I felt sorry for my stepmother when she arrived home. She was badly shaken by the commissar's threats. And I realized even more that she must not know about my plans, for if she learned anything she would be bound to report it.

Now came the problem of boots to replace those Jurek had taken. I went to Novo Sukhotino, but I searched the town for hours before I found some. They were high boots, up the calf and made of pigskin with rubber soles, my correct size, but as hard as stone. They chafed my ankles when I tried to walk but I overcame this when I found a pair of Jurek's discarded socks. Although the feet of these socks were reduced to a few threads, there was enough left to protect my ankles.

Every day now I visited Gunia to discuss our plans. We had no maps and still did not know exactly how we were going, but, knowing that Jurek had been seen at Novo Sukhotino station, we planned to go there and buy tickets for Kharkov. Gunia by now had her escape clothes ready, a grey woollen skirt, tall Russian boots and a warm coat that she had brought from Poland. Her head-scarves were similar to mine, but I was worried when she put them on. She looked nothing like a Russian even then.

April was drawing to its close but the weather was bad; for days it had been raining and it was cold. When it rained on April 30th, Gunia and I decided to put off our attempt for one day until May 2nd. On May 1st I went to see my mother-in-law; Kazik was not there and I told her of my plan. She cried, but she swore she would not tell a soul. Then she promised to give me food for the journey.

At three o'clock the next afternoon I visited her again and Christina and Czesia were with their mother. Into a bag I had made she put a piece of ham and a boiled chicken, bread and a tiny bag of money. From the bag around my neck I took a pair of gold ear-rings and a silver bracelet. The bracelet I gave to Czesia and the ear-rings to Christina. They thought them wonderful but only accepted them after giving me more money. Then it was time to say goodbye. Everyone was in tears, the girls wished me God-speed and my mother-in-law blessed me.

I asked my mother-in-law to tell my stepmother in two days that I had gone; she promised to do this and there were more tears and kisses as I left. I made my way back to Gunia's house to wait for the night.

Quickly we checked the few things we were taking. Around my neck with the jewel bag I hung my silver Madonna in its frame between the two identity cards. I counted my money and slipped that in with the jewels. I had three hundred roubles left after all my selling and buying. Quite a lot had been spent on food in the previous two weeks, for I was now two months pregnant and had tried to build up my strength for what was to come.

Gunia had seven hundred roubles; I saw her fingers shaking as she counted it. We were both nervous and there were six hours to go before we could move. We laughed at silly things, we tried to make conversation but it failed. We did not talk of our plan, of what might happen; now the hour for action was near we dared not think of defeat.

For a long time we sat and not a word was spoken, daylight turned to dusk and the dusk to darkness. At ten o'clock Gunia spoke. 'Eugenia,' she said softly, 'we must go now.'

Silently we stole from the house, made for the edge of the village and turned off over some fields so that we should not be seen going in the direction of Novo Sukhotino. Two miles farther on we made back to the road. So far we had seen no one and not a word had been spoken. For the first half an hour my heart had been beating madly, but now it was settling down; the night was cold but dry, and I took deep breaths of the air as we hurried along the road.

Novo Sukhotino was in almost complete darkness, but we did not go through the centre. We worked our way around the outskirts. It was nearly midnight when we saw the black outline of the station. We stopped, looked around to make sure we had not been seen, then silently crept the last two hundred yards.

CHAPTER VII

The Journey to the Urals

We crept through the gate and on to the platform. We could see the outlines of people but no one spoke to us, and were able at last to pick out about twenty persons. Most of them were lying asleep on the ground with bundles beside them, but they seemed to be in a sort of a queue leading to a small ticket office.

Without a word we went to the end of the queue and sat down. My heart was pounding again, but we could see no guards, no soldiers. It was cold and I was shivering. Now we could only sit and wait for a train going north, take our chance at buying a ticket and hope that we could board the train unnoticed.

Three o'clock came and we dared not move, some of the people around us began to stir and I caught snatches of their conversation. They were asking each other which trains they were waiting; some were going south and only a few appeared to be waiting for a train north.

Then came a noise in the ticket office. The clerk had arrived and two or three of the waiting men went to the tiny hole in the glass front. We still did not move; everything had to be left until the last minute. We could not chance anyone asking questions then and we sat waiting, listening.

A man near us was talking loudly; we listened and my heart nearly stopped beating. The northern train, to Penza, was due at four o'clock, the man said, but there had been a telephone message from the previous station that only two tickets were available.

Gunia and I looked at each other, but we did not say a word. We knew we could only wait and gradually the queue began to move. It was nearly four o'clock; the train was almost due, and there were still ten people in front of us when we heard a shout from the ticket office: 'No more for Penza.'

I could have wept at that moment. We were defeated before we had started. The train arrived a few moments later. Every carriage was packed and an attendant was calling for the two people who had been lucky enough to get those tickets.

We sat on the ground and watched the train draw out; I was too full of despair to say a word. If I had opened my mouth I am sure I would have cried. Gunia was silent, too; she looked as near to tears as myself when I glanced at her. Silently we got up and walked out of the station; there was no other train north until the following day. Nothing more could be done until then.

Into the town we walked and bought some food. We wandered into the market. There at least, we thought, we could meet people who knew the latest news from home. We saw a Polish woman who came there every day to sell second-hand clothes; I had spoken to her many times before and she called a greeting when she saw us. We stopped; there was nothing else to do. And as she talked I suddenly caught my breath, for she was telling of a Polish boy she had met in the market two or three weeks before. He was escaping she told us and had asked her where he could stay the night. I asked her what the boy looked like and she said he was tall and blond with a ginger beard.

It was Jurek, I knew; there could be no doubt. I asked the woman what had become of him. She did not know, but he had stayed at her house for the night, and early the next morning had left. She had not seen him since.

I offered up a prayer for Jurek, wherever he might be, for now I knew that he had got away from Novo Sukhotino. It gave me confidence that Gunia and I could escape, too, but we would have to plan things more carefully.

From the woman we got advice. We could never get away in the way we had tried that morning, she said. 'They will never give you a ticket,' she told us. 'There is only one way; you must find someone to get tickets for you.'

Tired from our night without sleep we made our way back to the village. My stepmother was waiting for me when I arrived home and from the set look on her face I expected trouble.

'Where have you been?' was her first question and I lied that I had spent the night at Gunia's house. 'I have heard that you are trying to escape,' stepmother stormed and she held out her hand. 'Give me your money,' she demanded, 'every bit of it. If you have no money you cannot escape.'

I did not know what to say or what to do; I could not give up money. 'I will give it to you tomorrow,' I said. But stepmother's eyes were piercing mine. 'Do you promise?' I knew I would have to lie again. I hated it and for seconds the words would not come. Then, dropping my head so that stepmother could not see the guilty look, I said, 'I promise, you will have the money tomorrow.'

It seemed to satisfy her, but I made my way at once to my mother-in-law. I told her what had happened and she was terribly worried. 'I have said nothing, but if your stepmother knows of your plan many others must know as well,' she said. 'If you are here tomorrow you must keep your promise to give her the money. You must go tonight.'

Suddenly she stopped, for my stepmother was at the door and already she was talking. 'I don't know what to do about Eugenia,' she was saying. One night she is here, another night she is somewhere else. I never know where she is and now she is planning to escape. I am worried about her state of health. When she lifts anything she faints.'

My mother-in-law tried to persuade her that there was nothing to worry about, but stepmother was now in a temper. 'The children are my responsibility,' she said. 'They have caused enough worry. Already I am in trouble over Jurek and I do not want any more.' She looked at me and I had to turn away. 'I expect you home tonight,' she said. 'There will be no more escaping in our family.'

I was upset, but the thought of dropping my escape plan was impossible. I looked around my mother-in-law's house. I imagined my child in those conditions and I felt sick. I went to Gunia's house, and burst into tears as I told her the story. 'We must go tonight, somehow,' I sobbed. 'Whatever happens, I cannot stay here any longer.'

Gunia tried to soothe me; she knew that my stepmother would have to report our plan if we did not go soon. She promised to leave with me that night and asked me to stay at the house whilst she went to find a friend.

In twenty minutes she was back at the house with her friend Boris, a Pole who had come on the same train with us from the Ukraine and had worked there for the Russians before he was arrested with his family and exiled. He was one of Gunia's few friends in the village and in the summer I had seen them out walking together. We sat down and Boris tried to work out a plan with us; several seemed workable but each time we came to the same conclusion – we must get tickets for our first break from Novo Sukhotino. For hours we talked until Boris had an idea: he knew a man who worked on the railway, and the man might be able to help. He would go to see him. For two hours we hardly spoke a word as we sat waiting for the return of Boris. We dare not hope for much, but this was our only chance.

Immediately Boris came back we could see that he had been successful. For fifty roubles, he told us, the railway worker would buy us tickets. We must not go near the station until the train arrived, but Boris would go with us to meet the man and collect the tickets.

Neither of us knew the railway worker, but through Boris he gave us advice on how to make the journey west. Never, he had said, get out of trains at main stations. It would probably take weeks to get tickets to take us farther if we did and the police would surely catch us as they regularly demanded papers at main towns. We were to book to the main towns, but we were to leave the trains at small stations before them. In this way it would be easier to obtain tickets and there would be little chance of meeting trouble. We gave Boris the fifty roubles and off we hurried again, promising to be back before nightfall. He still did not tell us who the friendly Russian railway worker was, but we gathered that he made his profit on the tickets and had managed to do the same thing for others in the past.

Again we had to wait and every minute seemed an hour. I was scared that my stepmother would come for me, for it was now dark. Just before midnight we heard someone at the door; I was so sure that it was my stepmother or Jasiek that I nearly cried out. But it was Boris who entered the room. Everything was arranged, he said. We must hurry, he said; we must start for Novo Sukhotino at once.

For the second time we stole from the house. Again we made a wide detour, not daring to go near my house. At the end of the village we took to the fields and we met no one. It was deathly quiet on the road when we reached it again and we took the same circuitous route around Novo Sukhotino to the station. Near the station was the huge elevator where months before I had unloaded the grain; around the elevator was a wooden fence and Boris whispered to us to hide behind it. 'Do not move from here,' he instructed. 'You must not be seen. I will come back with the tickets.'

Boris crept away into the darkness and down we crouched behind the fence. It was very cold again; here was almost open country and the wind blew through us from the fields. A few hundred yards towards the town I could see the dim outline of the blocks of flats where the town officials and security police lived. I shuddered as I thought of the dozens sleeping there who would have loved to arrest us. Neither of us dared speak a word.

An hour went by with no sign of Boris; it was three o'clock and I was cramped and cold. There was still no sign of movement anywhere, but now a hundred crazy thoughts were rushing through my mind. Perhaps the railway worker was not getting the tickets and it was a trap; perhaps Boris had been arrested; perhaps he had lied to us and would never come back; perhaps the guards were already looking for us. My stepmother might have raised the alarm.

Dawn was breaking, slowly and so pale at first. It was nearly four o'clock and still no Boris. We heard voices and movements from the station. Surely the train must arrive at any moment and it would leave again without us. I was nearly frantic from the suspense and felt that I could not crouch behind the fence a moment longer. Then, suddenly, Boris was beside us. 'Hurry!' he whispered. 'Here are the tickets, they are for Kurgan, a day's journey north but still in Asia. It would have been too suspicious to ask for tickets farther, they were the best the man could do.'

Just as silently as he had come, Boris led the way to the entrance of the station. Already we could hear the train in the distance; he had timed it perfectly. Boris hurriedly whispered the last instructions: 'Make sure you do not leave the train at a main station.' He wished us goodbye and God-speed, turned and disappeared behind the station. We wanted to thank him but we had no time. We waited a moment until the train was almost in the station and then we walked on to the platform.

I looked around but I saw no guards, no police. Again about twenty people were waiting on the platform, but only eight of them moved as the train drew in. There were ten seats vacant and we had tickets for two of them; I clutched them in my hand. Gunia lowered her head, for it had already been arranged that I should speak if we were spoken to.

Brake blocks screeched as the train came to a halt; it was full, we could see, and an attendant jumped from the train to call, 'Who's for Kurgan?' We hurried towards him. 'We are,' I said, and we were hurried to coach number nine, where there were two reserved seats, the only ones vacant. The coach was packed. Whole families, it seemed, were in it; most of them had come from Karaganda, the industrial town to the south, and they all seemed to know one another. They were singing or playing chess and draughts; we worked our way along the centre aisle and the people moved to let us into our seats.

Gunia slid herself in first; I wanted her to be nearest the window so that I could do any necessary talking. For what seemed an eternity we sat terrified, but no one spoke to us or even seemed to notice us. From outside came a shout and with a jolt the train moved forward, gathered speed and I saw the last houses of Novo Sukhotino pass out of view. We were still too scared to move or to talk; for a long time we sat like dummies, and my heart would not stop pounding.

In half an hour I saw the conductor making his way along the coach and I quickly nudged Gunia to turn her face and look out of the window. The conductor stopped. Without a word I handed him the tickets. He looked at them and said, 'Kurgan. That's not far. I will let you know when we get near,' and passed on.

Still Gunia and I sat perfectly still, even afraid to talk to each other. It was not until six o'clock, when the conductor made tea, that we moved, and when he reached us I bought two cups. The tension seemed to relax a little with the tea, but still I could not believe that we would not be caught. I searched every face around me, wondering who was this man, who was that. Any one of them could have been a secret policeman, I thought, but no one spoke a word to us.

At eight o'clock we stopped at a small station and I saw a boy on the platform carrying a tray of food. It looked wonderful to us, meat pies, sausage rolls and biscuits, such food as I had not seen for months. A great hunger gripped me; I opened the window and bought pies and rolls, biscuits, anything I could see. Half the food I passed to Gunia, since neither of us had eaten since the previous morning, and we both felt famished. We ate and ate until gradually my nerves quietened and I began to relax.

At eleven o'clock the train pulled into Petropavlovsk and my heart began to beat madly again as we stopped. Police, rifles with bayonets slung from their shoulders, were everywhere on the platform, looking at tickets as people boarded the train. Others walked up and down looking into the coaches. Gunia dropped her head at once, pretending to be asleep and I turned my head away from the window and leaned back with my eyes closed. For ten minutes we sat in agony; at any moment I expected to hear a shout and feel the rough hands of the police on me.

At last the train started and gathered speed. We were through the first main town. All through the afternoon the train stopped and started at the small stations, again we saw the food on trays and again we bought it and ate ravenously. In the evening the people opposite spoke to us; they were from Karaganda; they told us of the terrible heat there in the summer and asked where we came from and where we were going. They had boarded the train at Petropavlovsk and it was easy for me to lie. 'Just before Petropavlovsk,' I told them vaguely and said that we were visiting friends at Kurgan.

One of the men asked me if I played chess and I told him that I knew only the game of draughts. Immediately, from a bag he produced a draught board and we played for a long time until he asked me who had taught me the game. I told him 'my brother', and smiled as the man said: 'He taught you well, you nearly beat me.' Jurek had been an expert; many times he had

kept us alive by his skill at draughts and chess. Now I was more
at ease; others in the coach were becoming friendly. But I was
still terribly worried, for this was only the first stage of our
journey; less than two hundred miles separated us from Novo
Sukhotino and we were still well within Siberia.

I was thinking of the next stage of the journey when suddenly
I found myself clutching Gunia's hand. Down the coach walked
the conductor. 'Next stop Kurgan,' he called. We looked at
each other and my heart sank. We had made our first mistake,
our ignorance had taken us past the last small stations. It was
now too late. We would have to leave the train at Kurgan, a
large town – police and recapture.

Five minutes later the train began to slow and through the
window I saw houses standing three parts under water. Fields
for miles around were flooded, for the River Tobol had burst its
banks. The train squealed to a stop and the conductor called to
us. There was nothing else we could do; our tickets would take
us no farther. We had to get off the train.

Kurgan station was large and dirty. Hundreds of people with
their bundles were sitting, lying or standing all over the platform. Through the gate we could see hundreds more squatting
in the streets. The whole town seemed to be on the move from
the floods.

And then we saw the police; dozens of them were mixing with
the crowds and all carried guns with bayonets. The civil police
wore all-blue caps, but there were just as many railway police
with their blue caps with scarlet tops. Much later Gunia and I
had our names for them – cornflowers or poppies – but now the
sight of them sent a shudder of fear down our spines.

Into the main hall we hurried; hundreds more people lay
there with their bundles and we found a space to sit down among
them. For nearly an hour we sat, only our eyes moving as they
followed every policeman who walked through the crowds. I
prayed my thanks as none came near us; mostly they were keeping order among the people who had been waiting at the station
for days in the hope of getting a train.

I edged my way to the ticket window and asked for two
tickets to Kharkov, many hundreds of miles west, but the man
shook his head. I thought of Ufa, just across the Urals we

G

wanted so much to cross, but he shook his head again. In desperation I asked for tickets to Chelyabinsk, the next town, but the man in the ticket office stopped me. 'There will be no tickets west for at least a fortnight,' he said. 'You will have to wait your turn with the others.'

In a state of despair I made my way back to Gunia and told her. We were both almost in tears and the woman beside us, holding a baby, saw it. She leaned across; everyone was trying to go west from the floods, she told us, and most had already been waiting two weeks and they had almost abandoned hope of getting a train. But she thought she could help: if we took tickets back east, she said, we would be able to book westwards from a small station. We felt better; we could only hope that the woman was right, for the advice was similar to that given us before we left Novo Sukhotino.

There was no train back east that day and we settled down to wait in the large hall. Some food we had with us, and, carefully watching the police, I went to the refreshment kiosk at the other side of the hall and bought more food, tea and lemonade. Whenever the police were near we put our heads down and feigned sleep; not once did they speak to us and gradually a little confidence returned.

Spasmodically through the night we slept, but never both at the same time. We took it in turns, and always one of us was on the watch. As dawn broke I went to the ticket window again and asked for two tickets to Petropavlovsk. The man gave them to me immediately; there was no difficulty on this train and when it came in at four o'clock we found it was almost empty.

The train was about to pull out before we moved, then we hurried from the hall and climbed into the nearest coach. The few police around at that hour were sleepy and took no notice of us. We sank into our seats and sighed with relief as the train pulled out.

When the conductor asked for our tickets he stood for several seconds looking at them. He looked down at us and we felt again that this was the end, 'Only Petropavlovsk?' he asked. 'That's not very far.' He stood over us for what seemed an age, but I could not say a word. Neither of us spoke as he walked away.

It was half an hour before I left my seat and made for the toilet. Suddenly I stopped, for in the narrow corridor between the coaches stood the conductor. He was watching me and I could not pass. I stood rooted to the spot in fear, as in a dream I heard the conductor's voice. 'You are not a good liar,' he was saying. 'I know where you come from; Poland. You are escaping.' I felt I would fall and grasped for the hand rail. Then I felt the strong hands of the conductor holding me and I heard him whisper: 'Don't worry, I will not give you away. I've seen thousands of poor devils like you out here.'

I looked up at him. He was tall and reminded me of Jurek and he smiled in a kindly way. I told him everything; how we had escaped and how we had got off the train at Kurgan. Gently he put his hand on my shoulder, 'I, too, am from the Ukraine,' he said. 'My family lives near Zhitomir, but I work for the Russian railway and am away from home for weeks at a time. On this trip I am going as far as Omsk.'

The conductor promised to help. 'Three stations along the line,' he said, 'is the village of Malino. It is quiet and you should see no police. We will be there in an hour and then you must buy tickets for Koziol.' He told me that Koziol was the last station before Kharkov and was even able to tell me the number of the bus which would take us from there into Kkarkov. At Kharkov we must try to get tickets to a small station near Kiev, the conductor told me, but it was difficult to buy tickets to take us farther west to the Polish border. From there we might have to make the 150 miles or so by road.

I should have written down the name of the town near Kiev, but I felt so relieved at finding a friend that I did not think of it. The conductor talked to me for most of the rest of the journey. 'Don't worry,' he reassured me. 'You will pass as a Russian.' Then he looked at Gunia. 'It will be more difficult for your friend,' he said. 'She hasn't a Russian face and she will have to keep it hidden as much as possible. I think it better if she acts a mute and says nothing.'

We came to Malino. It was still very early in the morning and the station was deserted. The conductor bade us farewell and wished us good luck. We were alone, but his friendly wave gave us new confidence. On the tiny platform there was a wooden

bench and we sat down to wait. We must have been there for
nearly two hours before other passengers arrived and soon the
platform was quite full. We had not seen one policeman when
the tiny window of the ticket office near us opened.

First in the queue, I asked the girl at the window for two
tickets for Koziol. She told me that she was not allowed to do
this as Koziol was too near Kharkov and she could not issue
tickets to main towns. Chaguyev was the nearest to Kharkov we
could book to, she told me. I bought the tickets, not knowing
where Chaguyev might be, but thankful to get any ticket at all.

No one had asked for our identity cards and I had bought
tickets for a journey of more than two thousand miles. The sun
was shining and it was a wonderful day. Soon after eight o'clock,
as the train approached, we stood up and walked towards the
edge of the platform. Suddenly Gunia grasped my arm; I felt
afraid but I pulled her on. I too had seen a policeman at the gate
of the station, but the heavy hand on our shoulders did not
come. The policeman must have been sleepy at that time in the
morning, and when I next looked for him he had gone.

The train was crowded; a conductor showed us our seats and
again Gunia sat nearest the window. She turned her face away
as I handed up the tickets; we heard the conductor say,
'Chaguyev? That is a long way. The train does not go as far as
that. You will have to change at Penza. I will tell you when we
get there.' Neither of us spoke a word.

I felt sure we had aroused no suspicions and we settled down.
At the next station I bought food and milk, and Gunia and I ate
a huge breakfast. Later in the morning three boys boarded the
train and were shown to the seat opposite us. Within minutes
they were talking to us and we found that they were students
from a Moscow University. One was Russian, one was Polish
but born in Russia, and the third was a Mongol.

We soon found they were strictly Communist but they were
pleasant to us. The Russian told us they were studying to be
engineers and when he graduated he wanted to build fine
houses in Siberia. We listened as the Mongol said he was going
to build bridges in Mongolia, and we all laughed as the Polish
boy said, 'I do not mind what I build. I want to make a lot of
money.'

Gunia said nothing; she just nodded if they spoke to her, and it was not long before one of the boys quietly asked me, 'Why is your friend so quiet?' It seemed cruel to Gunia, but I had to make an excuse. 'She is not quite right in her head,' I whispered back. 'It is better if we do not talk to her. It worries her.'

For a long time the boy looked at Gunia before he whispered to his two friends. Then he leaned across to me again. 'It is a tragedy,' he said softly. 'She has such a lovely face.' They did not talk to Gunia again.

All through the day the train took us through the empty steppes. Not a tree to be seen, not a house for miles beyond the tiny villages. I found myself shuddering as I looked out of the window. We were still in Siberia and still many miles from freedom.

The boys asked where we had come from and I lied that my family had been in Novo Sukhotino all their lives. We still wore our scarves and the boys believed me. They joked about them and asked, 'Why don't you take them off? All you people from Siberia are afraid to show your hair. Or are you bald?' We laughed again but I did not remove the scarves. Gunia dared not: her blonde hair would have given us away at once. Not a tiny piece of it did she show and she spent most of the day sleeping or pretending to sleep.

Gunia, it was decided, would sleep on the seat where she sat, while I climbed on to the luggage rack above and stretched out. The boys made themselves comfortable on their own seat and luggage rack and gradually everyone began to doze. I longed to take off my scarves, for my hair was now damp and sticky. I waited until the lights were dimmed, then I pulled off my thick headdress and shook out my long hair. I untied the two plaits and massaged my scalp until it tingled with relief. I had been waiting for this moment for so long that in my ecstasy I could think of nothing else. Then I realized I was not alone; the boys were watching me and one of them was joking. 'So you have hair,' he said. 'We thought you wore a wig. It is beautiful. You should not keep it covered. There is plenty of time for that when you marry and have children.'

Suddenly I wanted to cry, they had been so nice to us. I wanted to tell them all, of my marriage, my escape, and the baby I carried. But I dared not, I knew. I tried to smile and said, 'No, it is not nice to show my hair.' That was the way the Russians talked; it was better, even if they were friendly, to arouse no suspicion. Eventually we all fell asleep.

In the early hours of the morning we passed a huge town but there was hardly a house to be seen. Everywhere were huge factories and power stations, I had never seen so many in one place before. I asked the boys where we were and they told me that it was one of Russia's largest industrial cities. 'Most of our industry is behind the Urals,' they explained. 'It is safer from any enemy here.'

It was still early morning when we drew into Chelyabinsk; the boys had to leave the train and they wished us good luck as they prepared to go. 'I hope we meet again,' said the Polish boy to me. 'You must come to Moscow. A young girl like you should go to school and be educated.'

I laughed and told him I did not want to go to school any more. We waved goodbye. I was sorry they had to go; they had been kind to us and I had felt that I was back among civilized people whilst they were with us.

We settled down, expecting the train to move, but in a few minutes the conductor walked through the coach. There was a fault in the engine, he said. We would be delayed for two hours at Chelyabinsk and we could leave the train. Gunia and I looked out of the window: the station was the most beautiful I had ever seen, with eight pure white marble pillars supporting the roof, while the walls were of the same spotless stone. It looked more like a palace than a station.

We could see no police near our coach and opposite us was the entrance to a buffet. We were both hungry and decided to leave the train. It might have looked more suspicious if we had not done so, I thought, for most of the other passengers were alighting. Through the door of the buffet we walked and what we saw almost took our breath away. The lofty walls were in beautiful pink marble and great silky curtains of the same colour hung from the windows, whilst against the far wall was the buffet counter, its front wonderfully carved in the same shade of pink. On the counter was the most delicious food I had ever seen in one place – caviare, fried chicken, salmon, hams and other cooked meats, delightful salads and choice pickles. A feast for a king.

Our eyes grew wide as we saw the food; then we noticed the benches in front of the counter and the illusion was spoiled. They were church benches with kneeling stools still attached. They had been taken from a church to furnish the palatial buffet of a railway station.

We wanted to explore more of this amazing station; no police came into the buffet and we walked through the door into the next huge hall. It was the same size as the buffet, but this time the colour scheme was different; mauve walls, mauve curtains and a mauve marble floor made it just as breathtaking as the buffet, but this was just a waiting room. At the far end was a flight of wide white marble stairs and our curiosity led us towards them. We climbed them and at the top came to the most ornate restaurant I ever expect to see. Again it was marble, but now of pale green; great pillars rose from the floor to the tremendously high ceiling, and even the tables were topped with the same pale green marble while the crockery was of the same shade.

We made our way down the stairs again. In our rough Russian clothes we could not eat there: it would invite suspicion, since obviously this restaurant was for the wealthy soft-seat passengers. Back to the pink buffet we went to the cold food. From plate to plate we wandered and ate until we could eat no more. It was a meal I was going to remember, and a long time was to pass before I saw such food again.

We still had a long time to wait and decided to see the town. No police were at the station entrance and here an official told us to keep our tickets. Otherwise, he said, we would not be able to get back into the station again. Outside we expected to see a beautiful city, but the sight which met our eyes was shocking. The town was dirty, ruinous and dowdy; the people were almost in rags and everywhere they queued for food. The only thing they could buy, it appeared, was hard yellow bread. The children looked thin and weak, and some of them cried to their parents for food.

It was too much for us, and we hurried back to the station. So this was Chelyabinsk, and being on the main Moscow to

Vladivostock line the station had been built for propaganda purposes. Inside was all the beautiful food in the world, but outside there was none. And without tickets the people of the town could not get into the station to buy food.

All through the morning we waited; our train was not going on, we were told, and we would have to wait for another. It was midday before it arrived and we were thankful to settle down in a seat again and wait for the miles to slip past.

On the next eighty miles to Zlatoust I began to recognize some of the places we had passed going east over a year before. Then in the late afternoon, after we had just left the tiny town of Miass, I suddenly caught sight of the Ural mountains in the distance.

I wanted to cry out for joy, for once we were over the mountains and away from Siberia the main barrier to our escape was overcome. I grasped Gunia's hand. 'Look, Gunia,' I said quickly. 'The Urals! Isn't it wonderful?' Gunia jumped up and looked into the distance. She held my hand tightly; I saw there were tears in her eyes and I wept too.

'Gunia,' I said, 'I want to kneel down and pray to God to get us safely across the mountains.' Gunia gripped my hand tighter. 'Don't, Eugenia,' she whispered. 'If we kneel we shall be discovered; everyone will know who we are.' We stood at the window together, our eyes closed, both of us praying silently.

From then on I could not leave the window. Soon I could see the tops of the Urals clearly and there was no snow now. Then I saw the first real trees for over a year, the sparse bare trees of the mountains. But to me they were beautiful; I watched them until it was dark and I could see them no more. Then I tried to sleep on the luggage rack again. But I was too excited; I slept little that night.

I was awake and it was still night when we reached Zlatoust in the heart of the Urals. We did not stay long and I fell asleep soon after we left. Now we were gradually nosing our way into European Russia.

CHAPTER VIII

Trainride through Russia

The morning was sunny and hot, but how different it was in the coach from the cattle truck of a year before. I was happy, but I was also hungry again, ravenously hungry. Tea and food we bought on the train, and when we stopped at small stations I bought milk. This meant more than anything to me; we had had so little milk in Siberia and now I looked on it as the main thing to give me strength.

As the day wore on I got more and more excited. First I saw houses with red roofs; then we passed close to trees, beautifully green. I recognized them as cherry and apple. I was so excited that Gunia had to tell me to stop pointing at every new thing I saw. I saw birds, too, and storks flew so close to the train that I could see their eyes. My eyes filled with tears, for in the dark despair of the Siberian winter I had thought I would never see such things again. I had prayed to die; now I prayed to live.

Dusk and darkness came again. It was time to sleep, but I could not. I was sitting beside Gunia, softly crying; it must have been the strain of those first few days. I felt a hand on my shoulder and looked up to see the coach conductor there. We were sitting just in front of his tiny compartment and I had noticed earlier that he was watching us closely. As soon as I saw his face I knew that I had nothing to fear. He was dark and Ukrainian. He squeezed my shoulder gently and whispered. 'Don't cry. I know who you are. I will try to help you.'

He squatted beside me and as he talked I stopped crying. 'I know where you are from and you are trying to escape,' he said. 'You would not harm me, I know, you're just children.'

I saw that his face looked sad. 'It's little better for us,' he went on. 'We have lived this life for so long that we are not human now. We are like animals. We cannot even look each other in the eyes any more.'

He left us, went into his compartment and brought us tea. For a long time he stayed with us and as the dawn was breaking he told us that the most dangerous place for us would be Ufa. 'The guards will come on board,' the conductor told us, 'but they will not search every coach. They will ask me if I have anyone strange on board and it is my job to tell them if I have.'

The conductor nodded his head down the coach. 'I have you,' he said, 'and there is a boy. But don't worry, I will not give you away.' He looked at Gunia and said: 'It will be better if you cover your head as though you are asleep.' Then he looked at me. 'You must pretend to sleep too,' he said. 'I will cover you up. I don't think the guards will disturb you.'

The conductor left us. It was getting light and it was time for him to make tea for the passengers. But before he went he put his hand on my shoulder again and whispered in my ear. 'Don't cry,' he said. 'You will draw attention to yourself. In Russia we don't cry any more.'

At midday we pulled into Ufa. Like Chelyabinsk it was another propaganda station, beautifully built in white marble. But now he had no wish to see what was beyond the station. Gunia pulled her persian lamb collar up around her face to hide it, drew her scarf low and turned into the corner as if asleep. I put my head down too, leaning on Gunia; the conductor pulled a blanket over us just as the train was stopping and gave me a reassuring pat on the shoulder.

Many of the passengers left the train as more got in and through my half-closed eyes I watched as several men walked along the centre passage. None of them was in uniform, but for me every one could have been a security policeman. No one spoke to us or touched us, but my heart did not stop pounding as for ten minutes we kept perfectly still. Then I offered up another little prayer of thanks as the train began to move.

We were well out of Ufa before the conductor came to us again, and I thanked him. I asked if the boy was all right and the conductor looked away. He answered quickly before he passed on: 'The boy has gone,' he said. 'They took him. I did not tell them.'

Gunia and I looked along the coach. Three seats down a boy of about eighteen had been sitting and we had noticed the previous day that he appeared to be nervous. He had repeatedly jumped to his feet to look out of the window. He was tall and blond and we had been sure that he was not Russian. Now he had gone. I shuddered when I thought what would happen to him, and what would have happened to us but for the help of the conductor.

For four days more we stayed in that train and each day put another two or three hundred miles behind us. Always, when we were approaching towns, the conductor warned us to put our heads down and sleep and never were we questioned. Passengers came and left; some became friendly, but now if I was asked where I was from I would name a town on the western side of the Urals. We ate well, buying food at the stations and drinking tea made by the conductor. He chatted to us often and said that it was a pity we had not been able to book to a station nearer Kharkov. Chaguyev was a long way from the city, he told us; we would find it difficult to get there and the police eyed everyone on the roads with suspicion. To help us the conductor even tried to buy tickets to Kharkov from other passengers. But no one would sell and as on the fourth day we drew into Penza at three o'clock in the afternoon we still had only our tickets to Chaguyev.

Police were everywhere on the platform when we left the train. The conductor had time only to whisper 'Good luck' before I heard a voice ask him, 'Anyone strange on the train?' I took a quick look at the man who had spoken; he was in civilian clothes, a security policeman. We dropped our heads and hurried away.

The platform was packed with people carrying cases, sacks or huge bundles and we saw a long queue leading to the ticket office. With our heads low we edged our way into the queue near the wall and stood behind two men carrying sacks.

At last we were at the window; dozens in front of us had been turned away without tickets and I hardly put my face around the edge of the window as I pushed our tickets through. The man pushed them back with two other tickets, white and bearing the numbers of reserved seats. I heard the man say that the train would be announced on the loudspeaker and he gave us its number.

Through the crowds we worked our way, often brushing past police, both 'cornflowers' and 'poppies'. We kept close together and bent low so as not to show our faces and made for the large waiting room. The station was not modern like some we had seen, but old with red brick walls. Inside the waiting room the walls were a dirty white; people were scattered all over the floor, and sacks, cases and bundles lay everywhere. There was only one policeman at the door and none inside. We hung back until a batch of people were going through and mingled with them.

Safely inside we made our way to a corner, stepping over the bodies on the floor and avoiding the bundles until we found a corner with just enough room to sit down. Several loaded sacks lay there and we got behind them, I sank to the floor and was asleep in a few minutes. I was exhausted. Gunia kept guard.

I awoke with Gunia shaking me. I had been in a deep sleep and for a few moments I did not know where I was. The pungent smell of the people around me filled my nostrils; I was overcome by a terrible drowsiness and could not stir. The journey was beginning to tell.

Gunia was talking quickly; she was afraid. Whilst I slept she had walked on to the platform to buy food and had seen the police stopping people and demanding their papers. Two people, said Gunia, had been taken from the station under guard. 'What can we do?' she was saying. 'They will get us soon.'

I heard her voice as if in a dream, for I could not move. I murmured to Gunia, but I was not sure if it was my own voice speaking. 'I can go no farther,' I was saying; 'leave me here to die. Now that I am in the Ukraine again, nothing else matters. Let me die. Please leave me.'

Gunia was shaking me again, harder, and I heard a voice booming over the loudspeaker, announcing the arrival of a train. Vaguely I heard the word 'Kiev'. Gunia was speaking again, trying to pull me to my feet. 'Quickly,' she said; 'this is our train. Eugenia, you must try, you must try, we cannot give up now.'

Wearily I pulled myself to my feet, with Gunia holding my arm. I staggered out of the waiting room and towards the train. Then the sight of the police brought me to my senses. I could not have counted them, there were so many. Everywhere they were talking to people, looking at papers. We put our heads down and went forward, pushing and squeezing through the crowd until we managed to cross the platform. It was only the mad crush of people which saved us from being stopped. We got into the train and sank into our seats, holding hands tightly for a few minutes until the train moved. I remembered to murmur another tiny prayer, then I was asleep again, back in the world of deep, deep oblivion.

It was still early evening, but I knew nothing more until the early hours of the next morning. The coach was darkened, but Gunia was wide awake. She handed me a piece of bread and a meat roll and told me that all was well. Not a soul had come near us as I slept.

All through the day we sat, scarcely speaking, while the train went steadily on. The conductor seemed not to notice us and we bought food and milk when a man brought it through the train at a main station. Several times the conductor made tea, thick and black without lemon, sugar or milk, the Russian way. Each time we accepted it, but these were the only times he came near us.

Everything seemed normal in the coach except for one woman who sat near us on the other side. Gunia and I watched her for hours on end; she did not look Russian, but neither of us could decide what she was. She had greying hair, cut short and with a fringe; her head-scarf was not tied like the Russian women, it was well back on her head with the ends falling to the back of the neck and tied there. She was dressed completely in blue, a blue skirt and a blue woollen jacket, nothing unusual, but I could not keep my eyes from the woman's face.

At times she looked as though she were a mental case, her face twisted as though she were in agony. It twitched and her mouth moved in a peculiar twisting motion. Her eyes were staring, frightened, fixed on one spot opposite her for at least an hour at a time. She said nothing to anybody and sometimes sat so rigid that there was hardly a movement of her body. But her face was seldom still. It was a face I shall never forget; it lives in my memory now. I was to see that woman again after we left the train – in a prison cell.

Night came and I slept again. The train was stopping only at main stations and there was little to disturb us. I was recovering my strength a little, though I still felt very tired in mind and body. All through the next day we sat, knowing that the farther west we went, the more difficult things would become. At Kharkov, we had been told, police examined the papers of almost everyone. We would need all God's help and I spent a lot of the day silently praying.

By evening we were passing the moors which lie near the River Don, and we knew we were nearing Kharkov. Soon the conductor was shouting. 'Next stop Chaguyev,' he cried, and the train was slowing down.

There I knew would be more police and it seemed that the lights were glinting on bayonets everywhere as we came to a stop. We should be getting off now; our tickets took us no farther. Suddenly I gripped Gunia's arm as she was about to leave her seat. I could not move. I was petrified. 'We must stay on the train, we must chance it,' I whispered hoarsely. 'I know we shall be arrested if we get off here.'

Gunia sank back into the seat and I kept a tight grip on her arm. The conductor was busy seeing people on and off the train and he did not notice us. In a few minutes the train was on the move again and almost at that moment the conductor was standing in front of us.

'Your tickets,' he demanded and without a word I handed them to him. We had hardly heard his voice in the two days on the train, but now the sound of it sent a chill through my spine. It was raised and harsh; everyone in the coach could hear and was looking our way. 'Your tickets take you no farther than Chaguyev,' shouted the conductor. 'Why did you not get off there? You are breaking the law. You must get off at the next station.'

I pleaded with him that we were trying to get to Kharkov and offered to pay more money if he would let us stay on the train. But his face was red with fury. 'How dare you get me into trouble by staying on the train without a ticket,' he shouted. 'If you don't get off the train I shall call the police and have you arrested.'

It was useless to argue. The man was in a furious temper and the threat of police terrified me. Meekly I apologized and tried to tell him that we thought we could buy tickets from him. I did not want to get him into trouble, I was saying, but he did not listen. The train was already slowing and he had hold of my arm. 'Off you get,' he almost screamed. 'Off you get before I call the police.'

The conductor almost pushed us out of the train as it stopped. He was still shouting and I looked around terrified that a policeman would hear. But there was no policeman; apart from the few people who had got off the train with us, the station was deserted. It was small and I looked up at a notice on the wall. We were at Koziol, on the outskirts of Kharkov, the very place we had tried to book to but had been refused.

From here we knew that we could get into the city and I spoke to a man who had been in our coach to ask him the way. He had heard the argument with the conductor and I am sure he felt sorry for us, for he offered to show the way to the terminus where we could get a bus or tram to the city.

It was cold and pouring with rain and I could see the dim outlines of houses as we walked through the cobbled streets. We walked for only ten minutes, but we were soaked when the man stopped at a tiny shelter in the street and told us to wait there for the tram into Kharkov. He told us the number of the tram, wished us goodnight and disappeared into the wet blackness.

Soon the tram came and we boarded it. I asked for Kharkov station and the conductor took a few roubles from me. For half an hour we rumbled along; outside was dark and murky and the lights in the tram were dim. Now my head was beginning to swim; I was shivering as the tram pulled up in front of Kharkov station. Huge and old-fashioned, the walls were cemented and dirty; we walked up the steps and into a huge churchlike main hall. A mass of men, women and children were sitting, lying or jostling with their baggage and bundles. Soldiers waiting for troop trains were everywhere, but this did not worry us. It was the police we feared.

The wooden benches around the hall were packed, there was not an inch to spare as people sat sleeping or talking, and we pushed our way to a vacant spot near a wall. Then I collapsed; every bone in my body was aching, I was shivering uncontrollably. My head was throbbing and I could not see; my throat was parched and felt as if it had closed completely. I sank into unconsciousness.

I do not know for how long I lay there but when I recovered consciousness Gunia was in tears. My head still throbbed and I still ached all over; I was ill and was sure that I was going to die. I could not move and whispered to Gunia, 'Go on alone, leave me here, I shall die.' Every whispered word hurt my parched throat.

Gunia was sobbing. 'I can't leave you like this,' she said. 'You must get better, Eugenia, you must get better.' She took off her coat, rolled it into a pillow and gently put it under my head. I tried to thank her but the words would not come. I fell into unconsciousness again.

Gunia was talking to me when my eyes opened again. She had found a buffet and had brought me chocolate and a cool, lemon drink. I tried to eat the chocolate, but I could not swallow. I tried to drink but it would not pass my throat. Gunia went away and in a few minutes she was back with warm tea. Again I tried to drink, but again my throat would not open to take the liquid which would have helped me so much. My head and body ached more than ever and the cold from the stone floor pierced me. Again I begged Gunia to leave me. I told her I must die that night, but she would not go. She put her arms around me and came close to keep me warm. Soon I was unconscious again.

It was still dark and cold when next I woke. Gunia was close to me, softly talking. 'Eugenia,' she was saying, 'we must leave here. I've been told that early in the morning the police come to clear everyone from this hall if they have no tickets.' Weakly I asked where we could go, but Gunia did not know. I pleaded with her to leave me and go on alone. 'What does it matter if they take me now?' I said. 'I know I shall die soon.'

Gunia looked down at me and shook her head. 'If I left you here like this it would be like leaving a dog to die,' she said. 'No,

Eugenia. If you are arrested I shall be with you and be arrested too.' Then she stood up; she would be back soon, she promised, and disappeared out of the hall.

In less than half an hour Gunia was back; she told me excitedly that she had bought tickets and that we had to go across the road to another station for a train to Belgorod. Neither of us knew where Belgorod was, but Guna had been told that it was only fifty miles or so to the north. She told me that we would be safe there, took my arm and begged me to go with her.

With Gunia's help I staggered from the main station. It was only two hundred yards to the local line station but I know I could not have made it alone. Eventually Gunia was almost carrying me. She was stumbling under the weight, but she got me to a bench on the platform to wait the few minutes for the train. Somehow Gunia lifted me into the train. There were few people around; it was still long before dawn and the coach was almost empty. Gently Gunia lowered me on to a wooden seat, she put my feet up and I heard her quietly whispering, 'Go to sleep, go to sleep.'

I tried, but now it was impossible. Doubled up as I was, my chest began to hurt. It got worse. Sharp knives seemed to be stabbing through me whichever way I turned. Eventually I had to sit upright for the two-hour journey.

Three o'clock. It was still dark when we reached Belgorod. Somehow I managed to get from the train into the waiting room and dimly saw that the walls of the station were covered with paintings of the Russian revolution. Again we sat on the floor, for there was no room on the few benches. There were hardly any civilians around; the room was crowded with soldiers. Several of them spoke to us and I began to feel a little better. They asked where we were going and, when we told them Kiev, they pointed out that this was a small sideline, but we could make our way back to the main line for Kiev if we got to Bogodukhov. It was some sixty miles to the south again but west of Kharkov we were told. It seemed our only chance of by-passing Kharkov and Gunia begged me to find strength enough to go and ask for tickets.

I forced myself to the ticket office, but I could not book direct to Bogodukhov. I took tickets as far as we could go along the

H

line and when an hour later the train arrived we sank once again upon the hard wooden seats.

Hours passed and the train stopped dozens of times at tiny villages. It was dark that night when we stopped at a small station and we were told to get off. I tried to buy more tickets, but found that there was no train to Bogodukhov until the next morning. There was one long bench on the platform and, as there was nothing more we could do, we sat down to wait.

Gunia sat on the end of the bench and I sat on her left. On my left was an elderly man and on the other side of him sat an old woman. We were the only people on the station; the other few passengers who had got off the train had left and we sat in complete silence. The two dim lamps which were alight hardly penetrated the darkness.

We had been there for no more than ten minutes when we heard the sound of heavy footfalls. I looked quickly to my left and suddenly into the dim light of the lamp came the figure of a policeman with a rifle and fixed bayonet. Gunia's arm went quickly around me. I prayed that he would pass us, but he stopped in front of the old woman at the other end of the bench.

I felt Gunia stiffen. I wanted to get up and run as fast as I could, but I knew this would give us away at once. We sat like statues. This must be the end, I thought; how could there be a way out now? We were trapped in a tiny station miles from anywhere.

The policeman was talking to the woman, 'Where are you going?' I heard him ask her and I heard her reply: 'Bogodukhov.' The policeman asked to see her papers and I saw the old woman hand them to him. He put them close to his face in the half-light, handed them back and said, 'You cannot stay here all night. You must find somewhere to stay in the village.' The old woman got up from the bench and shuffled off into the blackness. The policeman was now standing in front of the man beside me. The same question was asked, and the man told him that he, too, was making for Bogodukhov. He handed up his papers, the policeman scrutinized them and the same instruction was given: 'You cannot stay here all night.'

Then the policeman was standing a foot away from me; Gunia's head was lowered, but I had to answer when he spoke to me. Bogodukhov was our destination, I told him, and then came the question I was dreading. 'Where are your papers?' he asked. I opened my mouth, but I could not speak. 'Your papers,' said the policeman again. 'Where are they? I want to see them.' I tried again, but for a few moments I found I was stuttering unintelligibly. I was looking at the policeman and I am sure he could see the look of fear in my face. Then I blurted out the words, 'I have no papers.'

We were alone with the policeman now. The elderly man had disappeared and not a sound broke the tension of the next few moments. The policeman did not move. It was as though he did not know what to say next. It seemed an age before he spoke again and it was just two words. 'No papers?'

I shook my head and again there was the terrible silence. Then I heard a grunt from the policeman. 'No papers,' I heard him muttering, and then he spoke again. 'This is most strange,' he said. 'I have had nothing like this before. Everyone must have papers.' He did not seem annoyed; rather he was perplexed. He did not quite know how to deal with the situation.

For a few moments he stood rubbing his chin, then he told us: 'Wait here and do not move. I must go to see my officer about this.' He walked away quickly and we could hear his footsteps hurrying towards the station entrance.

At once the thought was in my mind that we must run. I grabbed Gunia's hand and we ran to the station entrance. Just through the door we saw a small office and inside a light was burning. Over the door was the one word, 'Police', and I knew that we could not go that way. We looked around, but there was no other way out. For a moment we were like rats caught in a trap. Then I saw the glistening of the railway lines. I jumped on to them from the platform, Gunia followed me and we ran.

For an hour we ran, stumbling from one sleeper to another. It began to rain in torrents and we slipped and fell many times as the sleepers became soaked. We could not see where we were going; only the rails kept us on the track as we kept on running.

Suddenly Gunia cried out. She had fallen again and I heard the thump as she crashed upon the rail. I stopped and tried to help her, not knowing from where my strength came. I did not feel ill now. I could have run for many more miles, anything to get away from that policeman. But now Gunia was screaming, the strain of it all had overwhelmed her.

I begged her to stop, but she became hysterical. She laughed and she cried and I could not move her from where she lay. Gunia moaned and screamed again, then she laughed and finished in a fit of heart-breaking sobs. In the pouring rain I sat beside her, her head in my lap. There was nothing more I could do. I knew exactly how Gunia felt.

Now she begged me to leave her, but I refused. She cried out for the policeman to come and arrest her, but her shouts seemed to rebound on us from the pouring wet darkness. For twenty minutes we stayed there before she could move, and then I gradually got her to her feet and we moved again along the line, slithering and stumbling from one sleeper to the next.

It was a long time before Gunia stopped sobbing. 'I must give myself up to the first policeman we see,' she was crying. 'I would rather be shot than carry on like this.'

For another three hours we walked, stumbled and fell. Gunia could hardly drag herself along, but now she was quiet. Then dimly in the distance we saw lights and as we got nearer we could see the dark outline of a station. It was Bogodukhov. We left the line and crept up on to the platform along a low fence. We found the waiting room, a bench and collapsed on to it, exhausted.

The benches were like church pews and were arranged in lines facing the same way. About two hundred people filled them and most of them were still sleeping. Water dripped from our drenched clothes to form small pools on the floor. We were filthy and our hands and knees were bruised and scratched from the innumerable falls we had had on the railway line.

I was too tired to think of all this and almost at once my eyes were closing and I was falling asleep. Suddenly a gasp from Gunia brought me to my senses again. She was pointing in front of us and saying, 'He is looking at me, he is looking at me.' On a small platform sat a policeman, facing the benches as though he were a schoolmaster, but he was not looking our way. He was drowsing and his head had sunk low. I tried to quieten Gunia, but she leaped from the seat and hurried to the door and

out into the teeming rain. Up and down the platform she walked
or half ran. I went out and begged her to come in again. I was
worried that she would arouse attention. But she would not
listen. 'He is looking at me,' was all that she could say. Gunia
was still slightly hysterical and I had to leave her to walk in the
rain.

Dawn broke and still Gunia walked the platform. Police were
now moving about the station and I almost dragged Gunia into
the waiting room. Soon in whispers we discussed our next move,
for with daylight Gunia's nerves had quietened a little though
she was still sure that every policeman was looking for us alone.

We knew that at any moment the hunt might start in Bogodukhov and we both agreed that to try to leave by train would
mean certain capture. The railway line again seemed our only
hope and we decided to take it. But just outside the station was a
junction, where one line went to the right and the other went to
the left. We did not know which one to take.

Out of the station we crept and walked along the path which
lay beside the line. Then we crouched behind a fence and waited
until soon after seven o'clock, when a train drew into the station
from the east. Over the loudspeaker its destination boomed:
'Kiev', and we watched as the train drew out to take the right
fork at the junction. For another ten minutes we waited until
the station was quiet again, then we climbed over the fence and
set off down the line after the train.

For three hours we walked. Gunia still said little, but I could
see that she was feeling better. It had stopped raining now, the
sun came out and our clothes began to dry. I opened my coat to
let the breeze blow through my clothes beneath, they were as
wet as my topcoat, but they gradually dried and soon I felt
hot from the sun and the long walk.

We did not see a soul as we walked. On either side of us were
green fields and the trees had broken into blossom. Neither of
us had eaten since the previous day and when we eventually
saw a tiny house in the distance beside the railway we decided
to take the chance and ask for food.

A woman of about thirty, carrying a young baby, answered
to our knock, but at the sight of us she drew quickly back behind
the door. We must have looked terrible; we were filthy and our

clothes were torn and faded from the rain. I called to the woman. 'Please don't be afraid; we are tired and hungry and have only come to beg food.' The door opened again. Inside a small fire was burning and we were invited to sit beside it. The woman apologized that she had little food, but she boiled some milk and gave us bread which we soaked in it. She seemed kind and when she asked why we were walking along the line I told her of our escape. There was no point in lying now, I knew. If the woman wished, she could raise the alarm immediately we left.

But she was sympathetic and wanted to help. We thought of making for Poltava on the main line to Kiev, we said, but she knew of a tiny village much nearer where she thought we could get tickets. She told us to keep to the right, where the line forked again and said that soon we would come to a path beside the line. For nearly an hour we stayed with her until she suggested that we should leave. She apologized, but said her husband would be home soon. 'He would not dream of hurting you,' she told us. 'But if it ever became known that you had been here we would both be arrested. I will not tell my husband that I have seen you.' There were tears in her eyes as she opened the door. I heard her quietly say, 'God bless you, my dears,' and we were on our way once more.

Soon we found the path and the going was easier. Several times we had to sit and rest, but by three-thirty that afternoon we saw the village and the small station ahead. This was the main line again; Kharkov and its terror was far behind. I shouted for joy when I saw the village, but Gunia appeared to take no notice. She walked on silently.

I asked what was wrong and Gunia answered: 'Please do not talk to me, Eugenia,' she said. 'Soon I shall feel better, but only now can I sort out my feelings.' Silently we went on, but I was worried. I wondered what Gunia might do when she saw a policeman.

In a side street, as we got to the edge of the village, we found a tiny shop. On the counter were sweets, pastries and bubliczki on strings, a Polish delicacy something like cheese straws. It was the first time I had seen them since I left Poland and even Gunia smiled as I handed her some.

We bought lemonade and sweets to put in our pockets. Gunia was talking freely now; through the grime on her face she looked almost happy as we made our way to the station. Once she actually laughed at children as they played in puddles.

There were no police to watch us as we went up the steps of the red brick station to the platform. There were no more than fifteen passengers waiting, but they stared at us as we walked to the ticket window. I asked for tickets for Kiev but the man said this was impossible, the farthest he could book us was to Piryatin, four stations and a hundred miles east of Kiev. I begged him to book us farther, but the man could not help. From Piryatin we would have to go by road, he said. There were plenty of lorries going to Kiev which might give us a lift.

We did not have long to wait for the train, but in the meantime we found a toilet. We were so filthy that we attracted attention. We had no towel, but I found a piece of soap in my bag. The cold water refreshed me and we were cleaner; we could no nothing about our clothes, but I was not worried. We were now only a few hundred miles from the Polish border and I was feeling hopeful.

Soon we were on the way to Piryatin in an uncomfortable train, full of men drinking vodka and singing Russian songs. The smoke from their cigarettes and pipes filled the coach and again I had horrible nausea, but they were a happy crowd and did not interfere with us. We were thankful to be on the train at all. From the boisterous conversations all around we gathered that the men were labourers, and that they had signed government contracts to leave their homes and go anywhere in Russia to build airfields. And from what some of them said they were hoping to complete their first airfield in less than the scheduled time so that they would qualify for a bonus. Those who were boasting of this were the ones who drank most vodka; some were very drunk and as they passed the bottles around it seemed to me they thought the bonuses were as good as earned already.

On the opposite seat sat a man who appeared to be in charge of the whole party. We gathered that he was the government official who had toured the villages recruiting the men and they treated him with great respect when they spoke to him. He was tall and dark, with a broad brown face and blue eyes and wore a brown suit and a short waterproof jacket. He did not speak to us, but many times I found myself looking at him; obviously he was an important man among that crowd of labourers in the coach.

Night came, but it was impossible to sleep; the men did not stop singing and by now most of them had drunk too much. We heard the conductor call, 'Next stop Piryatin'; it was three in the morning and not yet light. I took my decision quickly and whispered to Gunia, 'Pretend to be asleep.'

We both closed our eyes and did not move when the train stopped. In a few minutes it started and it was at least ten minutes out of Piryatin before the conductor came to us. He spoke but we did not move; he shook my shoulder and I opened my eyes and rubbed them as though I had just awakened from a deep sleep. 'Your tickets, please,' he said and I handed them over. Gunia did not move, she was still feigning sleep.

The conductor was looking at the tickets. 'They are for Piryatin only,' he said. 'We have passed there and you should not be on the train.' He seemed kind enough and I quickly apologized. I feigned surprise, told him we had been asleep and had not noticed the station and asked if we could pay to go farther, as really we wanted to go to Kiev.

The conductor was explaining that this was impossible when the man opposite spoke. 'What's the trouble?' he asked. 'Where do you want to go, please? Can I help you?' I told him that we wished to go to Kiev, but we had not been able to obtain tickets. The conductor was now saying that we must leave the train at the next station, but the man in the brown suit and waterproof jacket quietened him. 'Leave it to me,' he said with a great air of importance. 'I can get tickets for anywhere in Russia. When we stop I will get tickets for Kiev for these girls. I will take the responsibility.'

The conductor must have known the man, for he was satisfied. I thanked the man, but he smiled and said it was nothing. He was glad to show his importance, and when I gave him fifty roubles he was as good as his word. As the train stopped at the next station he told us to wait in the train whilst he went to the booking office. In minutes he was back and handed me two tickets on which were printed the magic words 'Kiev'. They could not have been expensive, but the man did not hand me the change; I wondered why, but said nothing, for it was fifty roubles well spent.

From then on the man talked to us all the time, but I soon realized that he was trying to find out everything about us. He asked us where we were from and I told him Kharkov. He asked why we wanted to go to Kiev. I had, of course, worked out my story. We had been to see relations in Kharkov, but my mother had been born in Kiev and I had never seen my grandmother or my aunt. We hoped to stay a few days; we had been told of the wonderful sights in Kiev and we wanted to see them whilst we were there.

As soon as I said this I knew that I had made a mistake. He seized on my last few words. 'If you wish to see the sights of Kiev,' he said, 'I will show them to you.'

At eight o'clock that morning the train drew into Kiev whilst the man was still telling us of the wonders he would show us. He got his thirty or so labourers into a group and ushered us through the barriers with them. Two policemen stood at the barriers, but they did not move as we went through. It looked as if we were with the party and I heaved a sigh of relief when we got outside. There the man told us that he had to arrange accommodation for the labourers, but said he would be back at the station to meet us at three o'clock. He made us promise to be there and we agreed; we still did not know exactly who he was and we did not wish to create any suspicion.

Left alone we looked out from the huge, modern, sandstone station. In front of us lay the large square and it was full of traffic. For the first time I saw a trolleybus; it intrigued me that it did not run on rails and I decided that we would ride on one. We found one which would take us to the centre of the town. Up the stairs we climbed and sank into the soft, comfortable seats. We gazed out at the tall buildings, many of them taller than I had ever seen before. Above us towered the Kiev Opera House, a huge, grey, stone building, and on top of it we saw the large statue of, I think, a woman playing a Greek harp. From the Opera House we went along a broad road, and in the distance and up a hill we could see a huge park, stretching on both sides. On either side now were large modern shops and we got off the

trolleybus to walk and stare in the windows at goods I had not
seen for so many months.

There were cafés, too, so many that we did not know which
one to choose; they all looked so bright and modern. But we
were hungry, and we walked into the nearest, where the bright
tablecloths, the neat, white uniforms of the waitresses and the
chromium plating nearly took my breath away. We made our
way to a corner table, settled down and took off our top
head-scarves and jackets. I soon realized that everyone in the
café was looking at us; but they were smiling too and they must
have thought we were two village girls in the city for the first
time, for they were enjoying our excitement as much as we were.

The waitress, too, smiled kindly at us as we gave our order. It
came on beautiful flowered plates, the cutlery was glistening and
we breakfasted on scrambled eggs, warm fresh rolls, real butter
and milk. It was a meal to remember. We felt human again and
good; the mad dash over the railway line of a few days before
seemed an age ago and the smiles of the people in the café
blotted out all thoughts of the hard, ruthless faces of the police.

From the café we wandered along the line of shops. One was
crammed with delicious oriental sweets and chocolates, and like
children we went into the shop and spent a long time choosing
sweets. Afterwards we wandered slowly up the hill towards the
park, filled with a contentment and a happiness I thought I had
forgotten long ago.

The park is known in Kiev as the Krosczatik and it was
beautiful. From the top of the hill, green well-cut slopes ran
down to the river Dnieper. In all directions were marble statues,
pavilions, huge exhibition halls and colleges. We found an
empty bench with beautifully carved stone legs and a wooden
seat, from which we could look out over the old buildings of
Kiev with their tiled, black or green painted roofs. We were at
peace with the world and the world looked good from there.
The sun was warm and the sky cloudless, and we fell asleep
peacefully until early afternoon. All was still around us when we
woke, but we knew we could not stay longer; we had arranged
to meet the man at the station at three o'clock. We could not
be sure that he was a friend, but he was our only hope of getting
tickets to take us farther west. We decided to take the chance.

The man was already there, waiting, but the moment we saw him I felt we had made a mistake in keeping the appointment. He was no longer in civilian clothes; he wore a greenish suit buttoned to the neck, of the same material as army uniform, but I could see no insignia or sign that made it military. And he wore no hat.

He seemed pleased to see us, however, and told us of all he had done that day, getting his men accommodated. He described the meal he had had, told of a wonderful bath, and asked us: 'Why don't you work for the government. I can give you a job in a coal mine or as clerks in a factory.' He appeared to be genuine, but the thought was going through my mind that he must get commission for every worker he recruited.

Neither of us rose to his offer of jobs and he changed the subject. 'Now, what would you like to see, girls?' he asked. His mood was gay and gradually we felt more at ease with him. I told him that my mother had talked of the beautiful churches in Kiev and he laughed, 'Oh, you want to see the churches,' he said. 'They are museums now. We have given up our old-fashioned ideas, but you shall see them just the same.'

By trolleybus he took us to the Lavra, a walled town inside Kiev in which stood the wonderful churches and monasteries of old Russia. On the walls on either side of the huge iron gates were giant paintings, one of the Crucifixion and the other of the Baptism of Russia. I believe there was a date on this one, 996, but the painting was scarred by what looked like bullet holes. I then conjured up a picture of the Russian Revolution, but we were inside the gates gazing up at the fabulous buildings before my thoughts could take me too far.

On most of the churches the tall, onion-shaped towers still shone in brilliant gold and the pictures and mosaics on the walls took my breath away with their sheer beauty. The man saw our wide-eyed wonderment and tried to hurry us on. 'We keep these places to show our children what stupid things our people used to believe in,' he said with an air of importance. 'We don't pray to those gods any more.'

Exquisite works of art were all around us, but the man dismissed them as though they were of no consequence. 'We have found better uses for most of the churches in Russia,' he said again and again, and eventually led us into a small, wooden building about a hundred yards from the gate.

Inside the hut-like building maps of the Lavra and picture postcards stood on racks. I had been looking through them for a while before I noticed that another man was present and that our guide was talking to him. Then in the dim light I saw what the other man was wearing; he was in a uniform of the same greenish material but this one had shining buttons. I stopped as though rooted to the spot. I could hear snatches of the conversation and the second man was asking who we were.

I held my breath and strained my ears. I thought I heard our guide say 'Poland', and then clearly I heard him say, 'They have lied to me.' I heard no more, for Gunia had caught my hand and was tugging me to the nearby door. 'Quickly, Eugenia, quickly,' she gasped. She half dragged me to the gate a hundred yards away; then she ran through the gate like a frightened hare. There was nothing else I could do. I ran after Gunia, trying to catch her.

CHAPTER IX

An End to Freedom

Down the road ran Gunia and turned into an avenue of beautiful trees in full bloom, and I saw the fallen blossom under my feet as I ran after her. Into a main street we ran and past tall buildings and shops, across the street in front of a trolleybus and down a tiny side road. Gunia would not stop. For nearly half an hour I kept her in sight and then, suddenly, she stopped just outside a park.

I was breathless. In my stomach I had a terrible pain and when she stopped I walked the last hundred yards to where Gunia stood. She was shaking from head to foot. 'Why did you run?' I asked, but Gunia could hardly control her words. 'That man, that man,' she stuttered; 'he was going to arrest us.'

What would have happened if we had stayed in the Lavra I had no idea, but now I knew that any suspicion must be intensified by our mad flight. We had to get out of Kiev and it would be dangerous to go anywhere near the station. Into the park we went and sat on a seat. Soon it began to grow dark, but we did not know where to go. An old woman whose job it was to keep the park tidy came and told us that the gates were about to be closed and we asked her if there was any other station were we could catch a train westwards. My heart sank when the old woman replied that there was only one station in Kiev, the one we had left that morning.

As darkness fell we made our way back to the station, looking everywhere in case our guide in the green suit was near. In the main hall Gunia went to a corner and sat on the floor; she refused to move from there and watched every person who came through the door.

I was hungry, but Gunia refused to leave the station again; we both needed food and when Gunia was quieter I went out to find a café, ate a hurried meal myself and bought more for Gunia, but as I got to the corner of the station hall where I had left her I saw that I need not have hurried. Beside Gunia sat a young soldier; they were both smoking cigarettes and it seemed they were the best of friends. In contrast to the hunted and worried look she had when I left, Gunia was now smiling and completely at ease.

She beckoned me to sit down and introduced me by my Christian name. She already knew the soldier's story, but they went through it again for me. He had a big open face, was Russian and said he was returning from leave to Polish Ukraine. Gunia had not told him we came from there and the soldier was telling her how much he was looking forward to his return. 'I would like to take my mother there,' he told us. 'The people are so different. They are gay, the countryside is so beautiful and the girls dress so prettily when they go to church on Sundays.'

I could not imagine that there was much gaiety in Poland now but, making comparison with his own countryfolk, the boy was obviously impressed. Gunia led him on and asked more about Poland; he made it sound to us like paradise. From her meaning look I gathered what was in Gunia's mind and I said nothing. We both listened wide-eyed and then Gunia heaved a great sigh. 'How I would like to see this wonderful country,' she said to the soldier. 'I am so tired of Russia, but how can we get to Poland?'

'Only soldiers and their families can get tickets over the border,' he told us, but now we could see he wanted to show his importance. I was hanging on every word and then I knew that Gunia's plan had worked. 'As a soldier I can get tickets for you as far as Koresten,' the boy-soldier declared. 'They cannot refuse them to me.'

Gunia murmured thanks in a way which made the soldier's chest swell with pride. She held his hand for a moment and told him how kind he was to help us start a new life. She asked the number of his company, exactly where he was stationed and promised to visit him as soon as we reached Poland. How could she forget such kindness? And then she discreetly slipped some money into his hand for the tickets. The soldier leapt to his feet and promised to return in a few minutes. As he went through the door we looked at each other and began to laugh; Gunia had done a wonderful job. In spite of her dirty and torn clothes she still looked beautiful and had used every ounce of her charm to get us on the next stage of our journey.

True to his word the soldier came back with the tickets for Koresten, a hundred miles on and only fifty miles from the Polish border. I wanted to hug the soldier but again I left it to Gunia. We still had a while to wait and she sat holding his hand until I am sure his heart was completely lost to the girl he thought would soon be visiting him.

Now it was time for the soldier to go. He was taking a train to another part of the border and there was a tender farewell for Gunia. She kissed him on the cheek and we waved as he turned at the door for a long, last look at Gunia. Then he was out of sight and Gunia's arms were around me. She hugged me so hard that I begged her to stop; we were both almost beside ourselves at her success. Gunia was like a new woman; she was no longer the frightened fugitive, dashing crazily through the streets.

It was half past nine when we heard our train announced; it was packed and uncomfortable, but we did not mind. Not one policeman had come near us; a hundred thoughts of home were going through my mind. We were almost there, I felt. The train was full of army families on their way to join the officers and soldiers occupying Poland and none of them had been there before. I listened to the stories of what they expected and laughed quietly as one woman said she was sure they would all be murdered by the Poles. We still had the food I had bought in Kiev; bread, hard-boiled eggs and meat, and Gunia ate most of it. I was not hungry now; I was too excited even to sleep as the train chugged on through the night.

I was dozing for the first time next morning when the conductor came to us to say that Koresten was the next stop. We were near the border now and we dared not try to stay on the train as we had done before. It was six-thirty and a beautiful sunny morning when the train stopped, and we went to the waiting room to consider our next move. Gunia's soldier friend told us not to walk along the railway lines, for soldiers patrolled them near the border, but on the main roads we should be able to get lifts on lorries. We should try to make for the small border town of Korets and cross the border at night.

The instructions seemed straightforward and we did not wish to be seen in Koresten for fear of being questioned. From the waiting room window we could see up the line and half a mile away was a road running parallel with the railway. We waited another ten minutes until the station was quiet and then we stole along to the far slope, went down on to the rails and ran the few hundred yards before leaving them for the fields.

The grass was soaked with dew and my feet were wet within seconds. We came to the road and jumped the fence. Looking back we saw that no one was following us and we confidently set off along the concrete road at a smart pace. Just fifty miles to the border and beyond that another fifty miles to Rovno. I wanted to sing for joy.

Late that morning we came to a small village on a hill and called at a cottage for food. Two women, one young and one old, seemed friendly enough and when we offered them money they prepared warm milk and gave us bread. We wanted to rest for a while, but we had not been there long when three men of the house arrived. The oldest looked at us suspiciously and began to question us; I lied as much as I could, but I was frightened. Hurriedly we got up, saying we had arranged to meet a lorry for a lift and walked as fast as we could until the village was well out of sight.

All that afternoon and evening we walked; the road was almost deserted and we passed no more than a dozen people, mostly elderly men who were roadmending. Lorries passed about once every two hours; some were loaded with road-making materials and once an army lorry filled with troops passed us. But none of them stopped and we did not beckon them. I thought this too dangerous in view of the searching questions at the cottage.

By dusk we were tired out; alongside the road was a forest and Gunia suggested we should stay there for the night. I wanted to go deeply into the forest for safety, but Gunia was afraid we would be lost. So we found a hole a little way in among the trees, gathered large leaves and ferns to cover ourselves and tried to settle down to sleep. Within minutes it began to rain, and soon the water flowed in tiny rivulets into our hole until we were lying in a pool of water. Sleep was impossible; we just sat, soaked and cold. Every noise on the road we thought was someone coming to look for us; we were wretched and miserable and could only pray for the dawn.

With the dawn the rain stopped, the warm sun came up, but we were in a woeful state. Water was in my boots and my feet were sodden. I took off the boots and then my coat to let the air and sun dry the clothes beneath. Most of my clothes were falling apart and large holes were appearing; our journey had taken its toll of the poor Russian materials.

When we were drier we began again and after an hour we saw a roadmender working in a ditch near a roadside cottage. We asked him the way to Korets and he told us that first we would have to go through Novograd Volynsk, a town twenty miles from the border. But he was helpful; not far up the road, he told us, a small road went off to the left. This was a short cut to Novograd Volynsk and would save us at least an hour's walking.

We thanked him and set off again. We soon came to the side road and I saw that it was sandy and not hard like the main road. I sat down and took off my boots. The socks were useless now and I threw them away. I took off my large head-scarf and into it put my topcoat, boots and foodbag. Over my shoulders I slung the bundle, then I set off down the sandy road bare-footed and more comfortable than I had been for days, for now my boots were as hard as iron. Gunia did not take her boots off but she, too, tied her coat and bag around her shoulders with a scarf. Our clothes were drying now and we walked on and on. We passed a small village and then reached the main road again, where we turned left and kept walking. But soon, I knew, I would have to stop.

Some time in the afternoon we sank exhausted on the grass by the roadside. Near us was an old woman working in the ditch; a goat stood beside her and farther up the road we could see a house. I asked the woman how far it was to Novograd Volynsk and she answered that it was not far but we could not make it that day. I wanted to ask her more but a terrible weariness was upon me. I lay back on the grass and within seconds was asleep.

Darkness was falling when I was roused by someone shaking me; it was the old woman and her voice was kind and motherly. 'You must not go on tonight,' she was saying. 'I can see that you have been on the road for a long time and you are exhausted. Please come to my cottage. You can stay there until morning.'

I looked up at the woman and her old wrinkled face was smiling. I roused Gunia and we followed the woman to her cottage. The inside was neat and tidy and a fire was burning; there were two wooden chairs, a table and a sideboard with pots and pans. I wanted to cry as the old woman fussed around us, took our bundles and made us sit on the chairs while she went to the stove. Here was kindness I had not known for so long. She was cooking up a soup of goat's milk and semolina.

We had not eaten since the previous day and the old woman seemed to realize how hungry we were. She stood over us ready to fill our plates again as we finished the first helping of the wonderful soup. She did not press us with questions, but I knew we could trust her. We told her our story and her dear face was in tears as we finished.

Soon her husband came home; he was the roadmender for that part of the highway and was as kind as his wife. He warned us that if we went to Korets we would face almost certain arrest; there was only one way over the border in the town, across a bridge which was heavily guarded. We dare not chance this, said the roadmender; we must swim the river at night.

My heart sank as I listened, for I knew that in my condition I could not face the ordeal of swimming the river. I burst into tears; I told them of the baby I was expecting and the old woman gently put her arms around me. 'My poor child,' she said, 'stay with me. I will look after you until you have the baby.'

Through my tears I thanked her but I knew I could not stay. I must get to my father before I had the baby, I told them, and soon the old roadmender had worked out another plan. His son, he told us, drove a lorry and often went to the border south of Korets and through Shepetovka; he would be passing in a few days and perhaps he would help us cross the border at some other place.

They were trying so hard to help, and it certainly would have meant prison for them if we were discovered, but I was impatient to get moving. I thought of my baby and every day was important. We decided to set off again in the morning and try to get a lift on a lorry. Then we slept, on the floor but between beautiful white sheets.

Early the next morning we woke, refreshed and fit again. The old woman was already preparing milk and bread for us and they both came to the cottage door to see us off. In a bag she had packed more bread and a little goat's milk cheese; it was as though she were saying goodbye to her own children. As we left we heard her bless us with tears in her voice.

For two miles we walked along the road before we heard a lorry coming from behind. We turned towards it, the driver saw us and I knew we were lucky. As he stopped I saw that he was young and smiling, I asked if he was going to Novograd Volynsk and he answered, 'Jump on behind. I am going there. I will take you.' Thankfully we climbed on to the back of the lorry. Drivers were forbidden to carry passengers in the front cabin. Among barrows, picks, shovels and other tools it was uncomfortable, but to us it was more than we had hoped for. Novograd Volynsk was four hours' driving; it might have taken us days on foot.

Soon after midday we neared the town. It would soon be time for us to start walking again, I was thinking, when suddenly the lorry stopped with a jerk. A quarter of a mile up the road we could see police with guns and bayonets.

We had no time to be scared. The lorry driver's head was at the tiny window in the cabin. 'Get off and walk behind the lorry,' he said and I knew he was worried. 'Get into a side road away from the police, keep off the main roads and make your way round the town.'

As we jumped to the ground and dodged behind the lorry I heard the driver call: 'Keep to the smaller roads when you leave the town. There are troops everywhere.' He drove slowly on and we kept out of sight behind until we hurried into the first side road we came to.

For ten minutes we wandered around the small streets of Novograd Volynsk, an old Jewish town, full of merchants and shopkeepers who were having a difficult time under Russian rule. At a tiny shop we bought bread, there was no milk but the shopkeeper gave us water. We asked him the quickest way to Shepetovka and he told us there was no need to pass through Novograd Volynsk. A little way out of the town, along the way by which we had entered it, we would reach a children's playing field and a cemetery. Just beyond it, on the hill, was a cross-roads. 'Turn right there and wait on the hill for a lorry,' we were told. 'It is nearly fifty miles, too far to walk.'

As quickly as possible we got to the crossroads and began to walk towards Shepetovka. Several lorries passed us but none of them stopped. The sun was warm and we sat down on the grass to rest. It was so peaceful that we fell asleep and slept for two hours.

On the road again a lorry stopped to our wave. But the driver was turning off just along the road, he said; he could not help. In another ten minutes an old private car approached and the driver stopped at our wave. He was not going as far as Shepetovka, he said, but he could take us part of the way.

For twenty minutes we enjoyed the comparative comfort of the back of the car as the miles slipped away behind us. Now it was time to walk again, for the driver was turning off for a small village. And then a thunderstorm broke.

Nowhere near was there shelter; the lightning blazed across the sky in angry flashes and the thunder deafened us. Rain fell in a solid sheet and in no time the roads were flooded so deeply that we could not see the cobblestones. We could only go on. Off came our boots and we paddled our way along the road, two ragged and bedraggled figures, fighting our way through the storm.

At times the flood of water was so bad that we had to leave the road, and once we were forced to make a long detour round a farm which lay to our left, because the water was so deep. At last the storm passed and the rain stopped, but it was a long time before the water began to drain away and the roads came clear.

Late in the afternoon we reached a village and, seeing no police, we decided to keep to the main road through it. But the twenty minutes or so that it took us to pass through were terrify-ing, for everywhere people turned to stare at us, or pointed at us, and tiny groups gathered and we could hear them quietly jeering as we passed. Then two small boys began to shout and they ran behind us laughing; we did not know why, except that we looked so dreadful.

We hurried on as fast as we could and were thankful when the village was far behind. A mile or two farther on a lorry stopped, but the driver looked at us strangely. I explained that we had been caught in the storm. He looked us up and down for a few moments before he finally nodded his head, then gruffly said, 'Jump up behind,' and we were away. In minutes I was shivering and could not stop. The wind whistled through my drenched clothes and I was thankful when at last the lorry stopped. It was dusk and we were in Shepetovka.

In Siberia the people with whom Gunia had lived had often talked of relatives in Shepetovka. Now that we desperately needed somewhere to sleep, Gunia said we should try to find them. At shop after shop we inquired until, as we were almost giving up, a shopkeeper called an old woman who lived in a house near by. She remembered the people for whom we were inquiring, she said, and I heaved a sigh of relief. She directed us to a house in another part of the town.

We found the house. Now it was quite dark as we knocked at the door. A man opened it and we gave the name of the people we wanted. My heart sank as he shook his head. The family had left a long time ago, he said; he did not know where they were, but he was sure they were not in Shepetovka.

I dreaded another night in the open and pleaded with the man for help. I dared not tell him our whole story, but I begged him to let us stay until morning. For a moment he thought as he looked at us; he wanted to help, he told us, but we could not stay in his house. 'If you stay here I must report you to the police,' he said. 'That is the law.'

I was about to cry when he took my hand and led us to the back of the house, to another smaller building attached to the rear wall. 'Up there is a loft,' he whispered pointing to a ladder. 'There is hay and straw for you to lie on, it will be better than sleeping in the ditches. But you must leave early in the morning. In my house is a member of the Party and he must not know you are here.'

We thanked the man and climbed the ladder. From the

sounds we knew that he kept chickens there. We could not see a thing in the loft and groped around until we found some dry straw to lie on. The roof was too low for us to stand, so we lay down and tried to sleep.

I must have been asleep for a while when suddenly I realized someone was touching me. I cried out in fright, but Gunia's voice came through the blackness. 'It is me, Eugenia,' she whispered and drew close to me. 'There is someone else here besides us.' Her voice was frightened. 'I cannot stay here, we must go.'

For a few moments we stayed close together, hardly breathing, listening, but I could hear no other sound. Soon Gunia was convinced that we were alone, but we found it difficult to sleep. Tanks, rumbling along the road towards the west, passed near the house in their dozens, the noise did not stop until dawn.

Now it was time to go and we stole from the house without disturbing anybody. We made for the main road, where all was now quiet; not a tank nor army lorry could we see. Perhaps it was war, we said, perhaps soon we would be able to cross the frontier with the army.

It was still quiet as we left the last houses of the town. We saw a signpost to Slavuta and I recognized it as the first town across the border from Poland; the trains stopped there for customs examination and it was less than twenty miles from the border.

Unfortunately the signpost did not tell us how far we were from Slavuta and we knew that we must try to cross the border at night. We had no means of judging how far from it we were and we decided to walk on until we could inquire. But we met no one. An occasional army lorry passed us on the wide main road, on either side of which were woods. There was not a solitary worker, not even a roadmender.

On and on we went but soon the loneliness began to worry me; the sun was shining warmly, but I felt there was something wrong. Everything was deathly quiet except for the sound of our boots as we walked mile after mile. Suddenly I grasped Gunia's arm; there to the right, in a clearing about half a mile from the road, were army huts and tents. Tanks and lorries were lying under the trees and all around them moved soldiers.

We were in a military area, and it was clear why we had seen no civilians for miles. 'We must go back,' I told Gunia quickly; 'it is too dangerous to go farther.' Gunia could not see the danger. 'That is silly,' she said. 'The army will not hurt us. They have been helpful before. Let us go on to Slavuta, then we can decide when to cross the border.'

Gunia seemed so confident now and I reluctantly agreed. We walked on, but all the time a dull fear filled me.

Every half mile or so we saw more army camps among the trees; if the soldiers had seen us, they appeared to take no notice and after a while I gathered a little of Gunia's confidence. And so it was that when we saw a soldier lying on the grass a few hundred yards up the road we had no thoughts of running, no thoughts of hiding or turning back. We saw no danger. We walked on, ready to answer a friendly greeting.

The soldier stood up as we drew level with him. 'Good afternoon,' he said and I answered his greeting. We did not stop. Nothing seemed wrong, but the soldier ran in front of us, barring our way.

'Where are you going?' he asked and his face was set.

I smiled cheekily. 'It's none of your business,' I replied.

'It is my business, we are holding manœuvres here. Where have you come from?' The soldier had not liked my reply, his voice was raised.

'I've been to see my relations.'

'We have to know who is passing here. Where are you going?'

'We are going home.'

'Where is that?'

'Poland,' I answered, but now my heart was beating fast.

'Where are your papers?'

I pulled out the identity card I had been given in Rovno, and handed it to the soldier. He looked at Gunia.

'Where are your papers?' he demanded and now my heart was pounding. For seconds Gunia did not reply, then she said, 'I have none.'

'Strange,' said the soldier, but now he was jeering. 'Two girls wandering the border and one without papers.' Suddenly his eyes flashed at me. 'I know you,' he said, and I quickly answered, 'But I do not know you.'

I could not understand. How could the soldier know me? He

grinned into my face, an evil grin which made me back away; his voice was hard and his next words startled me. 'Oh yes,' he said. 'I know you. When I was a civilian I worked in the passport section of the Politburo.' He waved my identity card in my face and leered down at me. 'I know you,' he said again. 'I issued you with this identity card.'

I put out my hand. 'Please give it to me,' I said. 'We are late and must be on our way.' He moved as though to hand me the passport and then pulled it back again. His face looked cruel, and his eyes were half-closed as he looked at us. 'You are coming with me,' he said, putting his hand on the pistol at his belt. 'We want to know more about you two.'

Taking my arm he swung me round towards a gap in the hedge and pushed us both forward. He was no more than twenty-four and a private. I turned on him and pushed him away as he came near to me. He started to shout but we refused to move.

From the other side of the hedge came another soldier and I saw he was a sergeant. The soldier was trying to push me again, but he stopped when he heard the sergeant's shout. 'What are you doing with those women?' demanded the sergeant and I could see he was angry. 'Let them go at once.' For a moment I thought we were safe, but the soldier shook his head. 'I know these women,' he said as he stood his ground in front of the sergeant. 'It is my duty to my country to arrest them. They are spies.'

The sergeant was furious, 'Let them go, I say. You are always causing trouble. Leave them alone, they are doing no harm.' More soldiers were quickly gathering around, but the soldier who had stopped us was screaming, 'I know them, they are spies, it is my duty to take them to the Commanding Officer.' The other soldiers laughed at him. 'Spies?' they said. 'Why, this one is no more than a child. Let them go, you big head.'

Now the sergeant was exasperated and he shouted for order. The others he told to go back to the camp and then he turned to the soldier, red-faced with temper. 'Very well then,' said the sergeant. 'Make a fool of yourself. Take them to the Commanding Officer, but you will be dealt with if you are causing unnecessary trouble.'

The evil grin returned to the soldier's face; he drew his pistol and waved it up the road towards Slavuta. 'Walk,' he ordered, and now we knew that we had better obey. He walked behind us, insulting us with filthy words and calling us spies as we went.

A short way along the road I saw a horseshoe lying on the road and could not resist the temptation to pick it up. I stopped and bent down but the soldier saw something suspicious in my action. As I picked up the horseshoe he jumped back and screamed, 'I will shoot you if you don't put that down.' He thought I was going to hit him with it and the situation seemed so ridiculous that I laughed. 'No,' I said, 'I am not going to hit you so that you have something to charge us with. I have done nothing wrong and I don't intend to do anything now.'

For a quarter of an hour we were ordered along the road and then the soldier made us turn left into a clearing. At the far side was a newly built camp. Some of the buildings were of brick and others were of wood. Dozens of soldiers gathered around as we arrived and asked why we were there.

Our escort told them he had caught two spies and they began to laugh. He shouted something at them. I did not catch what he said, but the men were suddenly quiet at his command. Was this an ordinary soldier, or was he a political agent put among the troops to spy on them?

We were led to an office in the largest brick building. The soldier knocked on the door and I heard the voice call 'Enter'. Through the door we were pushed to an officer sitting at a desk. I saw the three triangles on his collar, red with gold edging; he was grey-haired, human and intelligent looking.

The officer asked why we were there and our captor told him he knew us from Poland and we were spies. He was about to say lots more, but already the look on the officer's face was one of distaste. He cut the man short. 'That will be enough,' he said sharply, 'you can go.'

The soldier left the office and the officer smiled as he turned to us. He beckoned us to chairs and asked where we were from and I told him the story that we were from Poland and had been visiting relatives I had never seen before. He listened sympathetically as I told him we wished only to get back to our homes, then he said, 'I understand, I am Polish too.'

Up and down the office he walked and I could see he was
wondering what to do with us. Eventually he stopped. 'I have
never had this sort of thing before,' he said. 'I am a soldier and
I have no power to deal with civilians, especially women.' He
smiled again. 'I do not know what to do,' he said. 'I do not want
to keep you here. I wish that foolish soldier had not brought
you.'

Obviously he was worried and he paced the room again until
another officer, tall, dark and broad and of the same rank,
entered. For seconds he looked at us, then we all laughed as he
said, 'What are you doing here, are we starting a women's
army?'

But our laughter quickly stopped. The grey-haired officer
explained the situation and said; 'What can I do? The whole
camp knows they are here now and if I let them go I shall be
reported. You know what the position is.'

It was a few seconds before the second officer replied. 'We
cannot deal with them, but we cannot let them go,' he agreed.
And then I felt my heart was stopping. I wanted to scream, but
somehow stopped myself as he said, 'I know, we can send them
to the police. If they have done nothing the police will let them
go. If they have done something wrong, the police can punish
them.'

The grey-haired officer must have seen the terrified look on
my face. He looked away from me and at the floor. 'He is right,'
he said quietly, 'but I would not like to see you punished. You
look just a child.' He looked at me again as though he were
asking for forgiveness. 'For my sake,' he said softly, 'you must
go to the police.'

A guard entered at his call. 'Take them to the police,' he
said. 'Tell the police we have arrested them and ask them to
deal with the matter.' I was searching his face as he spoke,
praying that he would still change his mind. He turned away
from us when he had given the order and avoided our eyes as
the guard ushered us through the door. In less than half an
hour we were at Slavuta police station.

It was a wooden building and we were escorted through a
door at the back. The room was bare except for a desk, one
young policeman in greyish-blue uniform sat at the desk and

another sat on top of it. The soldier explained that we had been arrested in a military area and quickly left. We did not move as the policeman at the desk took out a long sheet of paper. They both looked tired and disinterested.

One of the policemen explained that it was just routine, but he must question us. They spoke kindly to us and said that as soon as the details had been checked we would be sent home. I told the same story of visiting relatives in Kiev for the first of May celebrations: we had been with a party but had overstayed and had had to make our way back alone. We gave our names, ages and places of birth, my father's name and my mother's name and then I was asked the name and address of the relatives in Kiev.

This could be checked, I knew, but I had to continue lying. I gave a fictitious name of my mother's sister and a fictitious address. We were trapped, I was sure. I had started lying and had to go on.

The short questioning over, I asked one of the policemen if I could write a letter. He nodded pleasantly and gave me paper and a pencil. I then wrote a note to my stepmother in Siberia. 'My escape bid has ended. I have been captured.' Now I was choking back my tears. 'Please do not try to escape,' I continued. 'Your son will be taken from you if you are caught.' And then I added a last line: 'Perhaps you are safer where you are. I think there will soon be war here.'

The policeman gave me an envelope and told me to drop the letter in the box near the door, where it would be collected. He had no suspicions then and did not ask to see it. Much later I heard that it reached my stepmother.

That evening we were taken to another police building on the other side of Slavuta and the policeman who took us almost apologized as he explained that we would have to be locked up until the following day. Up the steps we went into a tall, brick building and along a short corridor where another policeman was waiting with a bunch of keys. He opened a door into a small, bare room and we saw five women sitting on benches along the whitewashed walls. We heard the key turn behind us.

I looked at the women. They were all in some sort of Russian dress, but somehow none of them looked Russian. Gunia and I walked to a bench but not a word was spoken; every movement we made was followed by five pairs of eyes. We sat down and the eyes were still on us, glaring, suspicious.

Then I recognized one of the women. I felt relieved and spoke to her, but she just stared coldly at me and did not reply. I could not understand, for she was the grey-haired woman with the fringe whom we had seen on the train from Penza to Kharkov, the woman whose face was constantly twitching. But now it was composed and still.

'Surely you remember us,' I said. 'We saw you on the train from Penza to Kharkov.' I tried to sound friendly but the woman's voice was as cold as the look on her face as she answered, 'I have never seen you before in my life. I have never been to Penza or Kharkov. I live near Slavuta.' Now I knew the women thought we were put there to trap them. I said no more and sat in dreadful tense silence.

It was a long time before the silence was broken, then suddenly one of the women spoke: 'Why are you here?' The words startled me, and before I realized it I was answering. 'We were escaping from Siberia but we were caught.' More questions were asked and we answered them. Gone were the looks of suspicion now; we were among friends. Except for the grey-haired woman with the fringe; she did not say a word. The other four were an officer's wife, Stephanie, an officer's daughter, and two women in the national dress of Polesie, the poor Polish province just north of Rovno.

The officer's wife was short, dark, and about twenty-eight. Stephanie was younger, perhaps twenty-four; I saw she was attractive, with a small turned-up nose. They all spoke Ukrainian, but the Polish accent was easy to distinguish.

Gunia and I were terribly hungry now and when a light was switched on from outside I banged on the door until it was opened by a policeman. We asked for food, but he shook his head; he was sorry, he said, but the food was brought from outside and he could get no more that day. All he could get us was water before the light over the door went out. Gunia and I lay on the scrubbed floor; only sleep could help us forget our hunger.

But I was still lying awake in the blackness when an hour

later I felt someone gently shaking me. Quickly the voice
whispered in my ear. It was Stephanie. 'Quiet,' she warned. 'I
do not want the others to know I am talking to you, but I want
to give you advice.'

Quickly she questioned me. 'Have you told the police the
truth, that you escaped from Siberia?' I told her I had lied and
said we had come from Poland. Stephanie was so close now that
I could feel her warm breath on my ear. 'It will be better if you
tell them the truth,' she whispered. 'They will find out eventually and for months you will be dragged from jail to jail. We all
lied and we have been waiting here for four weeks.'

Stephanie stopped and we could hear the heavy breathing of
the others. No one was awake and Stephanie went on: 'If you
tell the truth, it will mean a quick trial and a prison sentence of
one, two or five years. But the prison for short terms will be in
Ukrainia. It is better than being in Siberia, where you do not
know for how long you are sentenced. The old grey-haired
woman, I think, was trying to escape west too, but she has been
lying. They are sure to find out and punish her more.'

I wondered why Stephanie was being so helpful, then she
whispered: 'I know your friend, I have seen her in Poland.
Where do you come from?' I told her and she gave my arm a
gentle squeeze. She told me her village; it was three miles from
where I was born and brought up. From that moment there was
a bond of friendship between us.

For a long time I lay thinking of what Stephanie had said. It
could only be a matter of time before checks were made in
Kiev; I had known that when I had lied to the policeman.
When the truth was known I might get a heavier sentence for
the trouble I had caused, and a sentence over five years, I
knew, meant a labour camp in Siberia. Before I fell asleep, I
decided to tell the truth as soon as possible.

CHAPTER X

The Questioning

Next morning breakfast was brought early; my stomach ached with hunger, but all I got was a small piece of bread, a piece of sugar and a mugful of black Russian tea. We had hardly finished when the door opened again, a police guard stood there and he beckoned to Gunia and me. 'You must come to sign your statement now,' he said and we were led across the town back to the wooden police house.

The same two policemen of the day before were there and they smiled in a friendly way when we arrived. They told us we had little to worry about. 'If this is the truth your case will be heard in about a week's time,' one of them said. 'The sentence should not be more than a month or two and then you will be able to go home.'

They pushed the typed statements towards us. What the policeman had told us was, no doubt, true, if the statements themselves had not been lies. Everything would be discovered, I was sure. Stephanie was right, it was just a matter of time and the consequences would be worse.

For a few seconds I stood with the pen in my hand. Then I put it down and looked at the policeman who was sitting at the desk. He was still smiling, but his brow furrowed as I spoke. 'I cannot sign it,' I said. 'I have lied to you. I did not come from Poland. I have escaped from Siberia.'

The policeman opened his mouth as though to speak but closed it again and stared at the statement. He turned to Gunia. 'What about you?' he asked and Gunia replied, 'I am the same. I have escaped from Siberia.'

For a full half-minute neither of the policemen spoke; they looked at each other and I could see they were upset. One of them got up from the desk, walked round and offered us cigarettes. 'I am sorry for you both,' he said. 'We wanted to help you but now we cannot. You cannot be tried by us. Now you are political prisoners and we shall have to pass you over to the NKVD.'

They let us finish our cigarettes and talked kindly to us as we smoked. They seemed reluctant to take us away, but finally one of the policemen buckled on his belt and put on his hat. 'Come with me,' he said; 'we must go now.' The other policeman shook our hands and wished us luck, then we were led through the streets, stared at by the few people who were around at that early hour.

I had a shocking feeling of nausea and wanted to be sick as we came to a tall, brick building and went up the steps. The policeman thrust more cigarettes into my hand and said, 'You will need these'; then, like his colleague, he quickly shook our hands before we were shown into a bare corridor.

A large clock ticked away the minutes and I could feel myself trembling as the full realization of our position gradually worked its way into my head. I wanted to scream as a man suddenly appeared in the corridor beside us. He was dressed in a yellowish-khaki uniform with a pistol at his belt and the insignias on his collar were different from any we had seen among the army. Sharply he said, 'Wait here, you will be called soon,' and left as quickly as he had come. We were now in the hands of the dreaded NKVD.

In ten minutes the door opposite opened. Another man stood there and he was pointing at us. 'Come on, one of you,' he said and his voice was hard. He looked at Gunia. 'You first,' he said and Gunia went through the door.

For an hour I waited, sitting alone on the wooden floor and staring at the door opposite. But not a sound could I hear from behind it. I trembled until I was shaking all over. Suddenly the door opened and I saw Gunia; she was crying, her face and eyes were red with tears.

I was soon on my feet, holding Gunia's arm. 'What is wrong, have they hit you?' I asked, but Gunia shook her head. 'No, they have not hit me, but they are after something, you will see.' We had no more time to talk. The man was at the door and pointing at me. 'Now you,' he commanded. I walked through the door and it closed behind me.

The room was small and furnished as an office: a polished desk, a tall cabinet against the wall, four chairs and shelves piled high with papers. Out of the window I could see the low roofs of the town, but I looked at them for only a second. The voice said 'Sit down' and I sat on a chair to the left of the man at the desk.

I looked at him and saw a broad face with a wide upturned chin: his lips were razor thin and tightly pressed together. His hair was brown and greying at the sides and his eyes sent a shudder through me as I waited for him to speak. They were brown, glistening and cruel, eyes which pierced right into me.

His uniform was the yellowish-khaki of the NKVD and I could see he was an officer. At his neck was the insignia of a cross and he had a narrow belt across his shoulder and down to the wide belt around his waist which held a gun.

The first question came and his voice was as hard and cruel as his eyes. 'What is your name?' and I gave him my maiden name. 'Laessig,' I answered.

'Where were you born?' I told him and he asked when.

'Why were you sent to Siberia?'

'I don't know. You should know. You sent me.'

'Where is your father?'

'I don't know. You put him in jail.' Instinctively I did not say that father was in German Poland.

'Why did you escape?'

'In Siberia there was starvation. I am expecting a baby and I knew that if I stayed there I would die.'

The officer was annoyed and banged his fist on the table. 'Don't lie,' he shouted. 'There is no starvation in Russia.'

I felt afraid but determined he would not make me cry like Gunia. 'If there is no starvation why don't you go there.'

He was enraged. 'I don't believe you,' he roared. 'There is no starvation.'

He banged the table again and again. His piercing eyes were drilling into me and I gripped the sides of the chair. An evil grin came on his face and his voice was suddenly calm. He leaned across from his desk until those eyes were a few inches from mine. A chill went through me as I heard the slow cruel words: 'You are a spy, you were making your way back to Poland as a spy with information.'

He asked what towns we had passed through and what I had seen: he asked me who we had stayed with and I told him 'nobody'. His temper was rising again and his evil face was almost touching mine. 'Why have you been so long in getting here?' he rasped. 'Who were the spies you stopped with to get information for Germany?'

A sudden and new fear gripped me as I realized what was on the officer's mind. Quickly I told him we had talked to no one: we had taken a long time because we had walked far. Nothing I said did he believe. 'Why didn't you go directly west from Kiev?' He gave me no time to reply. 'You went north to meet other spies,' he said. 'Then you were trying to get across the border with your information.'

My fear was now changing to annoyance at his accusations. I looked into his face and found I was shouting too. I told him the villages we had passed through to the north. 'Why should I spy?' I demanded. 'I only wanted to get to my home, Rovno, and work like everyone else. I refused to stay in Siberia and starve and have my baby starve too. Siberia is another world, another planet: there are no trees, no food, just a slow death.'

Another officer entered the room as I was talking: he was dark and Mongolian-looking and leaned on the desk to grin at me. 'We shall find out all about you,' he said. 'If you do not tell the truth we shall send you to jail.'

I was still annoyed and I seized on his words. 'Do you give food in jail?' I asked, and the officer was still grinning as he replied, 'Yes, of course.' But his face changed when he found why I had asked the question. 'Good, then I will go to jail,' I shouted. 'If you give food there it is more than you gave me in Siberia. I will go to jail.'

For moments the officers did not speak. They looked at each other and then at me: they were wondering how to frighten me again. 'You don't know what our jails are like,' one of them said, and I could see how he was baiting me. 'We will send you up where the white bears are.' When I smiled and asked, 'How long?' the answer came, 'Ten years,' but they could scare me no more.

K

'I am only nineteen.' Now I was calm as I answered. 'When I come out I shall be twenty-nine: there is still time to have a good life in Poland.'

I waited for the explosion but it did not come; they had failed. They had not hit Gunia and I was confident now they would not use force on me. All they wanted was an admission that I was a spy and I was not prepared to give it. I would tell the truth, that was all.

For nearly two hours they interrogated me, but all I could say was that I had escaped from Siberia. In desperation they sent me away, but as I left the room one of them called out: 'That is all for now, my clever young woman. Tomorrow you will be back again, and you will again sign a statement.'

The NKVD soldiers took charge of us and we were taken back to the cell and the other five women. I needed rest. I was exhausted and nervous and I could see no way out of the situation; but it was a long time before we could satisfy all the questions the women asked and I was allowed to sit quietly with my own thoughts.

That a war with Germany was imminent I was now certain: I almost prayed for it to start – anything so long as I was saved from what I was sure was otherwise to come. But quickly I asked for forgiveness for my thoughts; war was too terrible.

I was still deep in thought when a policeman came into the room and asked Gunia and me if we had any sharp instruments or pieces of metal. For a horrible second I thought of my silver Madonna and my hand went protectively to where it hung at my neck. I could not bear to give it up. We said we had nothing and the policeman went away.

As the door closed I suddenly remembered my two identity cards; I had given the name of Laessig but still had the second one bearing the name Wasilewska. Somehow I had to destroy it. I called the guard and asked to be taken to the lavatory: then I quickly tore the second identity card into tiny pieces and disposed of it. Why I had not been searched already I could not think.

It was not long before I realized how narrowly I had prevented the discovery of the second identity card. In less than an hour there was the sound of a key in the door and a soldier of the NKVD entered. He demanded every paper we had. Gunia had none and I handed over the passport in the name of Laessig. At least the NKVD officer would have to admit that I had told the truth in one respect, I thought.

The other women looked on silently until the NKVD soldier had left. Then Stephanie told us what had happened to other girls who had been there before. Everything they possessed had been taken from them, she said, and my hands went again to the small bag still hanging around my neck. The jewels would go, of that I felt sure: but my silver Madonna, somehow I must keep it. Never before had I been parted from it.

High in the wall was a small window and I asked what was outside. One of the women knew there was a garden and quickly I took the Madonna from around my neck and pulled the tiny silver plaque from its frame. By standing on Gunia's back I could reach the window and I threw out the frame. If the guards did not see the frame, I thought, they would not be looking for what was in it. The Madonna I kept tightly in my hand from then on. I prayed that I could keep it somehow.

During the evening little was said and my thoughts turned again to escaping. Behind the lavatory I had seen a high wooden fence and when I had been there earlier I had heard footsteps and voices. There must be a road the other side of the fence, I could not stop thinking; on the other side of that fence might be freedom.

I dared not speak of this to Gunia; if escape were possible this way, I must attempt it alone. Suddenly I made up my mind and banged on the door. When the guard came I asked to be taken to the lavatory, outside the building. As before, I noticed the guard remained near the door of the building and at least ten yards from where I was going.

As I had remembered, the door of the toilet faced the wall, and looking round I found I could not be seen by the guard. I could just reach the top of the door and for a few seconds I hung there; gradually I pulled myself up until I managed to get a slight foothold halfway up the door. I turned myself round carefully until I was facing the fence, the top of which was no more than three feet away. My heart was pounding and I knew that I had not a second to spare. I jumped.

With a crash which jarred my whole body I fell to the ground, I had missed the top of the fence by at least twelve inches and I nearly cried. In a second I was up and reached for the top of the door again: I found the foothold and turned around for the second time to face the fence. I was lowering myself into a crouching position for the second jump when my heart nearly stopped in fear. The guard was shouting. 'What are you doing there?' he called. 'Why are you so long? Come out at once.' My heart began thumping madly. If I jumped and grabbed the top of the wall, would I have time to pull myself over?

At that moment I knew it was too late: the heavy footsteps of the guard were already coming towards the toilet, so I jumped to the ground and picked myself up a moment before he arrived. I burst into tears when the door closed on me a minute later; I had not been strong enough for the attempt and I felt terribly sick.

Next morning, after breakfast of black tea and bread, the guard came again for Gunia and me. To the NKVD building we were taken again and marched to the room we had been in the day before. I feared the worst as Gunia went through the door first.

I sat on the floor, expecting at least an hour's wait, and I began to think of the answers I would give if the same questions were shot at me again. But I sat for no more than ten minutes. The door opened and Gunia came out. Now it was my turn.

I heard the door close and saw the same two officers; but now they smiled as I entered, offered me a cigarette and I took it. I was ready with my answers and determined I would not admit to being a spy, but they were not needed. The officer with the greying hair was already speaking. 'I am sorry you are in trouble,' he said, 'but you are still a young girl and there is time for you to change your ideas.' He still smiled as he carried on: 'You have time to get out of your head the idea that people starve in Russia. You will find that we are all equal and everyone has the same.'

He put out his hand and shook mine. 'I wish you every success,' he said; 'you will now be sent to a prison to await your trial, and when you have served your sentence I hope you will be a good citizen of Soviet Russia.'

The other officer shook my hand. 'Every success,' said he. 'I am sure you will eventually be a fine citizen.' I wanted to laugh. Fine citizen! But I bit back the answer I longed to give; it would do no good to antagonize them now.

A statement was put in front of me and without waiting to read it I signed. I left the room and we were taken back to our cell. Stephanie was furious when we told our short story, 'Stupid, stupid, to sign a statement,' she said. 'They can write anything into it before your trial, far better to refuse and hold them up.' Gunia looked at me in horror. What had we admitted in our statements? Had we been tricked, had we agreed that we were spies. I felt wretched, and horrible nausea was with me again. I cried out for the guard, rushed to the lavatory and vomited.

Pains were shooting through my stomach and a dreadful hunger was tearing at me when at midday pea soup with pieces of meat floating in it was brought in. We expected nothing more that day and I ate my small portion ravenously, but late at night the cell door was opened again and a guard gave us a quarter of a loaf. He told us we were leaving and we were ordered out of the cell and in front of the building. There stood an open lorry: thirteen male prisoners were already in it and we were ordered to climb in too. Two guards with rifles and bayonets sat in the rear corners and into the night we drove.

The guards tried to stop us talking, but we soon found that the men were Polish. I do not know how it started, but I found myself singing with the others, as loud as I could, Polish hymns and patriotic songs. Even louder we sang as the guards tried to quieten us; they shouted but we would not stop. We were all cramped closely together and they could not move among us, so the lorry bumped on its way and our Polish voices went out into the darkness of the Russian countryside.

For twenty or thirty miles we jolted over the roads until we came to a town and pulled up in front of a railway station. I saw the name on the wall. We were back in Shepetovka.

From the lorry we were ordered into the station, a train was waiting there and it was full of prisoners. Every window was barred and the coaches were split into small compartments with barred doors leading into each. One of these doors was opened and the five women, Gunia and myself were ordered in.

But none of us could get through the door. From inside the carriage came ear-piercing yells and screams; a large piece of bread flew through the door and hit the guard in the face. He tried to push us in but someone was trying to push us out; it was pandemonium and I heard the guard shouting, 'This woman is crazy, no wonder no jail will keep her.'

At last the seven of us were pushed in and the door was slammed behind us, but the yells and screams went on for a full minute before I was able to see who was making the noise. She was no more than twenty-five and little more than five feet tall; her hair was short and blonde and her face was covered with freckles. And her voice was one of the loudest I have ever heard.

We sat down on the hard seats, the train began to move and at last the girl with the freckled face sat up in her corner and stopped yelling. Defiantly she glared at us and no one spoke, then suddenly she said, 'Why did you come in here and take the little fresh air that I had?'

None of us replied. We dared not, and it was Stephanie who began to laugh. Freckle-face must have been getting over her temper, for in a few seconds she was laughing too. Then we all laughed, except the woman with the grey fringe; nothing could make her laugh, and she hardly ever spoke a word.

We did not know where we were going or what was in store for us, but freckle-face had provided the relief we needed from our worry and we grasped the opportunity in our laughter. Soon she asked where we had come from and a dozen other questions and then we learned her story. Her name was Luba and she had been accused of stealing a pair of boots from her brother, an offence which might have brought her a one or two month jail sentence. But Luba had been kept in jail for eleven months awaiting trial; her brother had gone to work in Bessarabia, part of occupied Rumania, and he could not be found to give evidence. Luba could not be kept in any jail awaiting trial for more than three months and so she had been moved from one to another, three months here and three months there.

No wonder she screamed and threw things whenever she saw a guard; the long months were gradually affecting her reason.

Every prison guard knew her and was scared to go near her; she would do things that would have brought serious punishment to others, but Luba they left strictly alone.

With the coming of a new day we could see we were going south; time and time again the train stopped in open country, reversed and went slowly forward again. From the calls along the train we knew it was full of prisoners, men and women. And like us they were hungry; we had only the piece of bread we had been given the night before.

Once I banged on the bars and asked to go to the lavatory, hoping there might be some chance of escape. But there was no lock on the door, the guard stood outside and there were bars on the tiny window. I was escorted back to the carriage and gave up all thought of escaping as my hunger got worse.

Night came and still we were given no food; we banged on the bars again and screamed for something to eat, but it was useless; we got nothing. We learned that we were to have gone to a jail at Kamenets-Podolsk, a hundred and fifty miles south of Shepetovka, but the line had been broken and now we were being switched to a prison at Proskurov, just half as far down the line. There was no food on the train for us. We would have to wait.

CHAPTER XI

The Women's Prison

All through the night the train stopped and started, I could not sleep for the pains of hunger and thirst. It was daylight and about six o'clock in the morning of the second day when we came to the last stop. There were shouts outside; I looked out and saw a station but no town. There were only fields and woods.

One by one the carriages were unlocked and we were told to get out and line up facing the station entrance. In front of me were about thirty women and there were a few more behind me; in the rear the men were paraded, but I could not see how many there were. Guards of the NKVD were waiting for us and the order to march was given. We filed out of the station and the column moved slowly along a tree-lined and unfinished road full of large holes and inches deep in mud.

For about an hour we walked when suddenly I saw uniforms I recognized. They were Polish. Dozens of captured Polish troops were working at the side of the road and we called to them as we passed. They asked where we were from and I shouted, 'Siberia, where they have sent your families.' Boos and shouts filled the air and the guards waved their rifles as they screamed for order and made us walk faster.

Behind me I heard Stephanie and the officer's wife crying; somewhere, they knew, father or husband was a prisoner like these. Now the pace was quickened until we were almost running. The guards rushed us past the Polish soldiers and their shouts soon faded into the dim distance.

At eight o'clock we entered the town of Proskurov, marching through the centre as the townspeople stood staring at us with scared looks on their faces. In front of a large, three-storeyed building with white walls we were halted and I looked up to see that the windows were barred or covered with wooden shutters closing outward.

The huge gate was opened and we filed through. First we were counted and then the men were led away to the left of the yard. I followed the other women through a door and into a large bare room with whitewashed walls. It was May 24th.

Inside the room stood a middle-aged woman dressed in a long white coat and she looked at each of us as we passed through the door. Suddenly she saw Luba and started shouting for the guard, and just as quickly Luba started yelling. Again there was pandemonium as the woman screamed, 'If this one is coming back here, I'm going to leave. I can't stand her again.'

Luba laughed and yelled the louder until a guard pushed his way in and told the woman that Luba would have to stay; there was no other place for her. The woman shouted an oath at Luba, then she left us and at last Luba was quiet.

Out of the window I could see a huge square like a parade ground. It was our exercise yard, I was soon to discover, and in the far corner was a guard house from which armed guards paraded around the square close to the buildings. Luba pushed her way to the window and called to the guards; she knew every one by name and some of them began to laugh when they saw the freckled face. But Luba knew what to do; she yelled again at the top of her voice until the guards stopped laughing.

Luba, of course, knew the procedure for new arrivals. She ordered us to listen whilst she told us what to expect. 'We have little time,' she said. 'If there is anything you want to keep you must hide it now, for soon they will take everything you have, ribbons, shoelaces, money, jewellery, razor blades and anything else they can find.'

We were all wondering where to hide our belongings, but Luba was ready for our questions. 'Sew them into the linings of your clothes,' she said, and when we asked how, Luba again had the answer. She went to the small stove in the corner of the room and began to pull the paper out, behind the paper was an old stocking and in the stocking were hidden three needles.

Quickly we began to pull the stocking to pieces to provide the thread. I slipped the bag from around my neck and pulled the lining apart inside my coat. Under the shoulder pads I pushed my mother's watch and some brooches. I was about to do the same with a gold ring, beautifully set with diamonds and rubies in the shape of a crown, when Luba stopped me. 'Sew the ring behind the buttons,' she told me. 'They seldom find them there.'

This I did. I felt sure the thread from the stocking would be seen, but it was the only chance I had of saving anything. Piece by piece I hid everything in my clothes and then I came to my silver Madonna. I was in a panic. It was too large. It was sure to be found if I tucked it into the coat. I looked all round my clothes for a safe place. But there was none.

It was Luba who again came to my aid. She saw me holding the Madonna and looked down at my boots. 'Are they new or old?' she asked, and I lifted one foot to show the worn soles. 'Good, we'll hide it there,' she said. From another girl we borrowed a small butter knife and with Luba's help I prized the lower layer of sole from the next until the nails pulled away. Between the two layers we pushed the Madonna plaque, then I stamped my foot until the soles were together again and no gap showed.

Gunia had hidden most of her belongings in her coat as I had, but she still had three hundred roubles. But when she saw what I had done with the Madonna, she pulled off one of her own boots and prized open the sole. In went the notes and she stamped the sole back. It looked perfect.

Of the money I started my journey with I had only fifty roubles left and Luba told me that it would be better to give the money up. Receipts were given for it, she said, and although I was not allowed to hold the money I could buy bread, salt, fat, cigarettes and combs once a fortnight with the credit at the prison shop.

For two hours they left us alone and all the women were busy with the needles. Everything was out of sight when in came another woman in white, tall and hefty like a man, and asked us to give up anything we carried apart from our clothes. Many of the women passed things to her, but I saw there was little of value left after we had finished with the needles and thread. I passed over the fifty roubles and one brooch which was too bulky to hide. I was given a receipt, but I never saw the brooch again. Gunia gave up a watch which had belonged to her husband, but she kept a small prayer book in her hand. It had been given to her when she went to her first Communion.

Gradually we were all dealt with and the woman in white shouted, 'This way, we are going to clean you up now.' She opened the door and we were led into the large exercise yard. I looked quickly at the walls, but I saw there was no chance of escape that way; they were nearly thirty feet high and from inside we could not even see a tree. At windows on the far side of the yard we saw men prisoners staring at us, while guards patrolled all round the buildings.

Through a gate in the wall we passed into another smaller yard and lined up against a low, whitewashed building. The woman in white gave the order: 'Strip off and leave your clothes outside.' We had to undress in the open and I could see the guards peering through the gate just fifteen yards away, waiting to pounce on our clothes and search them.

Inside the building were showers – which were merely pipes with holes in them – and each of us was given a handful of strong green soft soap. In batches of ten we were ordered under the pipes and for the first time in more than a year I felt warm water streaming over me. It was a wonderful feeling and I appreciated it more than anything. But in two minutes we were ordered to make way for the next batch.

Then the woman walked along the line of women with a bucketful of a yellowish liquid, stopped at each one of us, dipped a jar into the bucket and poured the liquid over our heads. My hair was now down to my waist and she tipped two jars over my head and rubbed the liquid into the scalp until it hurt. It got into my eyes and made them sore; it got into my mouth, a foul and sour, vinegary liquid.

I looked around for something with which to dry myself, but the woman ordered us into the next whitewashed room, hot like an oven. We did not need towels. We were dry in a few minutes. At the far end of the room was another door: the woman opened this and a furnace-like blast swept through and scorched my skin. It was an oven and in a huge pile lay our clothes. The vultures outside had finished their search and now our clothes were being baked to kill any vermin which might have been in them.

When the heat cooled, our clothes were roughly pulled out and we were left to sort them out. Quickly I felt through the lining of my coat and my heart sank as I found that every one of the larger pieces of jewellery had been discovered and taken. But I had not lost everything. Mother's ring was still in its place behind a button and several pieces, like ear-rings, had not been discovered. Then I breathed a prayer of relief as I saw that the boot hiding my Madonna had not been disturbed. I left her in the hiding place for a long time.

Gunia had been lucky too: the money in her boot had not been found. But we had little time for talking before we were led out of the building and across the exercise yard again, through another door and into one of the tall buildings which formed the square around the yard.

The walls were clean and freshly whitewashed, the stairs were of stone but well scrubbed. At the second floor there stood a guard with a long list in his hand; the first door in the corridor was opened, Gunia's name was called and she was pushed inside with Stephanie and the officer's wife. Then I realized I was being separated from Gunia for the first time; we had been arrested together but now we were being kept apart so that we could not work out a story for our defence.

Gunia did not have time to speak or even to look round, the door was closed quickly and from then on I saw her only for a few minutes each day when we were at exercise. Along the corridor we went until we were stopped again outside another door, my name was called and I breathed a sigh of relief as I heard Luba's next on the list. I had known her such a short while, but in Luba I felt I had a friend; although she was strange at times, she was good-hearted and had been helpful.

Several other names were called, the door was opened and I found I was being pushed from behind. The door hit me in the back as it slammed shut and forced us in. Eight more were crammed into a cell in which there were already more than sixty women.

I looked around at the whitewashed walls, the high ceiling and the scrubbed, wooden floor. High on the far wall were two small windows and each was covered with the outward sloping boards through which we could see the sky but nothing more. In the far corner stood a rough wooden cabinet about three feet wide with a metal basin in the top. A small tap came out of the wall above it and under the cabinet was a wooden barrel with a lid. It served as the lavatory for us all and the stench from it was foul.

The door was wooden and heavy, with a two-inch peephole for the guard outside. Farther along the same wall, near the door, was another peephole in the brick.

Although the cell was no more than forty by thirty feet, seventy women were packed into it. All around the walls they squatted and in the centre of the cell sat another small crowd of women, back to back.

To move round the cell I had to step over the feet of the women in the narrow sort of pathway which formed itself between those in the centre and those against the walls. Beside each woman was a small and pathetic bundle of belongings and I took care not to tread on them as I edged fearfully around the centre circle until I found a small space. Gradually I forced myself down to the floor, squeezed between two old women. Then I heard women around me laughing and for a horrible moment I dared not look round, thinking they were laughing at me. But many of them had recognized Luba; she had been in the same cell before and they were soon asking her the news from outside and from other prisons. For a long time Luba kept them entertained with her stories until the noise was so great that the guard banged on the door.

At times I found myself laughing too, but now I had a terrible ache in my stomach. I had had nothing to eat for two days apart from the quarter of a loaf we had been given at Slavuta.

Nobody spoke a word to me and gradually I took in the scene. There were three classes of women in the cell. Against the wall beneath the windows were about six mattresses, just sacks filled with powdering straw, and the women sitting there were all young and under thirty. Against the wall opposite and near the door sat the old women. In the centre squatted a mixture of young and old, but already I could sense a sharp division between the women on either sides of the cell.

The younger women did not wear head-scarves and took no notice of myself and the two other newcomers, but some of the old women who did wear head-scarves were grinning at us as though they were gloating over the fact that we were there with them. I looked at the faces of those nearest the door: one must have been over eighty, the next one was terribly thin and pale, and the third had a cruel grin on her face as she looked across at me. In the centre of this line sat a huge woman who towered above the rest; my mind pictured her as a duchess and she acted like one as she ordered the women around her where to sit.

Some of the women became more friendly with time and I came to know every one of them, but now they were asking the usual questions. 'Where have you come from? Have you seen friends of mine. . . ?' and so on. And every quarter of an hour, it seemed, the guard banged on the door as the noise became too loud.

The two women from Polesie were sitting nearer the old women, and although I am sure they did not mean to harm me, I discovered later they had told the women that I had come from a wealthy family. It was some time before I realized it, but gradually I felt eyes on me. Many of the old women were looking at me with hate. I felt miserable and uncomfortable, and I tried not to look their way, but they still stared and whispered to each other until I felt I could scream.

At seven o'clock that evening there was a great shout, the door opened and a guard carried in a large bath-like bowl of dreadful-looking soup.

There was a mad rush to the cabinet and I was carried with the others; I grabbed at a tin plate and a round, polished wooden spoon with a very short handle. The bowl was placed in the centre of the cell and then I saw how life in the cell was lived, how the strongest survived and the weakest did not. From the group against the wall under the windows a girl stepped to the front and she was holding a large wooden ladle. She was short, pretty and blonde, and I later gathered that her name was Nina and that she was the widow of a high Russian officer who had been killed in Finland. She was the cell leader and she stood over the bowl, ladling out the soup. Those who were lucky got a dip from the bottom, otherwise the ladle was filled with thin, watery soup from the top. And Nina would take arguments from nobody.

'If there are any complaints come to me,' she shouted. One or two of the women tried to complain about the poor helping they had been given, but Nina silenced them with a blow from the ladle. She stood there, mistress of them all and she knew it.

Many of the women were much stronger in body than Nina, but later I found where her real strength lay. If there was trouble in the cell the other young women along her wall stood by Nina and the older women knew they had no chance in a fight. Nina was the leader and spokeswoman for them all. If there were grievances it was she who stood at the door and argued with the guards. I found that she had been in the prison for over six weeks; she had sold a radio which had been lent to her, and she still had many months of her sentence to serve.

At nine o'clock the single light in the wire cage over the door went off and I tried to sleep. But it was hot and the stench was dreadful. I tried to stretch out and lie on my back, but there was not enough room. Like sardines, the only way to lie was on our sides, packed tightly together, and soon I gave up trying and sat up. Then I began to cry. For hours and hours I cried and prayed, but I did not really know what I was praying for.

The next morning Nina came across the cell to me. 'Come over here,' she ordered. 'I want to talk to you.' I followed her to the wall and we sat down on one of the mattresses. 'What are you crying for?' she demanded and I nearly broke down again as I tried to answer her. Slowly I told her of the baby I was expecting and my fear of having it in prison, but Nina stopped me. 'Don't worry about the baby,' she said. 'When the time comes you will be taken somewhere to have the baby and you will be allowed to stay with it until it is six months old. Then the baby will be looked after until you finish your sentence.'

I felt a little better, but Nina was not finished. 'But don't cry,' she told me and I felt it was an order. 'We have no time for people crying in here.' She looked across at the women in the centre and on the other side of the cell and turned again to me. 'You stay over here with us,' she said. 'If you stay with them' – and she waved her arm across the cell – 'you will die. They will steal everything you possess. They hate you already.' She looked around at the young women on either side of her. 'We are known as the underworld of the prison,' she said, 'but we look after ourselves. You must join us and then you will survive.'

The other girls in Nina's gang were looking at me. They were thieves and prostitutes; one of them I learned was a murderess. All of them were young and strong, but they looked kindly at me and I knew I would be safe from anything if I stayed with them. Nina looked over at the older women opposite. 'They are crones,' she shouted, and several of the old women looked down under her glance. 'They care for no one but themselves. They would help nobody.'

Nina put her hand on my shoulder. 'This is not Siberia,' she said. 'There you were nothing, but here you are a citizen of Russia and we expect the same rights as anyone else, prison or no prison.' I did not cry again. From that moment I was accepted as a member of Nina's gang.

I soon discovered how good her advice was. 'If you want something, just yell until you get it,' she would tell me. 'If that doesn't work, go on a hunger strike. And if someone is about to hit you, hit first. It doesn't matter who he is, he will respect you for it.' She told me something else which I never forgot: 'Never sign a statement,' she said. 'No matter what they say to you, never sign.'

All that day I stayed with the gang and most of the time I sat next to the wife of a Polish doctor. She was the oldest of the gang, had been arrested at Shepetovka while trying to return to Poland, and told me how terribly worried she was. When she was arrested her one-year-old-son had been taken from her and she did not know where he was. I almost forgot my own worries as I listened to her story. 'The baby is all I have in the world,' she told me. 'When I get out of here I shall be too old to have another and how shall I ever find my baby again?'

It was not long before I found out more about the other women. The old and thin woman beside the opposite wall had been sentenced to fifteen years and was awaiting transfer to a labour camp. She had bought materials and made head-scarves to sell, and had been arrested for profiteering. A Jewish woman of about forty-five, named Sara, had bought matches and sold them at twice the price; she had been sentenced to ten years. But a young girl who had killed both her parents with an axe, because they objected to her marriage, was serving a five-year sentence.

When night came and we began to settle down, Nina and her friends edged out slightly and made room for me on a mattress. The older women noticed this at once and across the cell came the shouts: 'Why is she on a mattress. You have to be here three months before you can have one.' In a second Nina was on her feet, hands on hips, glaring across at the older women. 'Who said she has not been here three months? If anyone wants to say she has not, let her stand up now.' No one moved, no one spoke. Nina sat down again, but from the other side I could hear muttering.

Soon afterwards the prison governor came to call the roll and stood just inside the door with a guard behind him. He had just finished calling our names when one of the women from the other side went to him 'Look,' she said, pointing at me, 'she has just arrived and already she is sleeping on a mattress.'

I held my breath, expecting trouble, but Nina and her friends were ready for it. They leapt to their feet together and began to shout. 'Lies,' they cried, 'she is telling lies. The girl has been here over three months. It is all lies.'

The governor did not want to hear more. He left and we heard the key in the lock and his footsteps fade away. Then as one Nina and the girls acted. They rushed at the woman who had spoken to the governor. As quick as lightning a blanket was thrown over her head to muffle the screams and they began to beat her unmercifully. At the same time the other girls started to sing and shout at the tops of their voices until, in a few seconds, the guard hammered at the door, shouting: 'What's going on in there, what are you singing for?' From out of the deafening din a voice called back: 'We're singing because it is such a lovely night,' and the beating, the singing and shouting went on until it was thought the unfortunate woman had had enough. Then the light over the door went out in an attempt to quieten us and the noise died down. There was not another murmur in that cell that night.

Nina and the gang looked after me until gradually I became accepted, but still many of the older women, I could see, did not like me. When the food came – bread and tea for breakfast, soup

L

for dinner and supper – Nina always saw that I got a good helping from the bottom of the bowl. If the others raised a murmur, one wave of the ladle quietened them.

In a few days Nina persuaded me to take off my head-scarf, and sometimes the girls combed and arranged my hair in plaits or other styles. They treated me almost like a doll. I was the youngest in the cell.

At half past ten every morning we had twenty minutes exercise in the big yard and there I saw Gunia. We always tried to walk together and Gunia told me she was in a tiny cell with fifteen others. They were friendly to her, she said, and one girl had just arrived who had relations in the Siberian village where we had lived. She was able to tell Gunia that my stepmother had received a letter from Jurek, but she knew no details of what he had written. At least Jurek was still free, I thought, and I offered up a little prayer of thanks.

When I told Nina that my friend was in the next room we decided to make a hole through the wall so that we could speak to her. One of the girls had an old spoon handle and for hours we scratched at the wall until we got so deep that the spoon handle was not long enough. Gunia and her friends were scratching from the other side but we never found out how thick the wall was.

Early each morning we were taken downstairs to a lavatory and wash-room where there were three taps and we lined up to wait our turns. Some of the girls were lucky enough to have had money to buy soap, but there were no towels and to dry ourselves we had to use our own clothes, vests, petticoats or anything we were fortunate to have kept. Most of my clothes were by now so rotten that they were useless and I was pleased that the weather was warm and I did not need them. But one of the girls had hidden a needle in a piece of soap and I had begun to repair the clothes during the long hours in the cell.

On the sixth morning the time came for the floor to be washed. All the women took turns to do this and the other women pressed against the walls as it was done. So far I had not taken my turn, but this morning, when the bucket was brought in, one of the older women eyed me from across the cell.

'Why doesn't "The Lady" wash the floor?' she called out and I could sense trouble. 'I suppose she wouldn't know how to do it. Her kind never have to wash floors.'

I stepped forward at once.

'I don't mind washing the floor,' I said, but the woman laughed at me.

'Your type is not fit to live,' she jeered. 'How would you know about washing floors?'

Nina and her friends stood back and did not move as I went to the bucket and started work. Every eye in the cell was on me as I scrubbed all down one side of the cell, and the older woman (she was about forty) walked over the wet boards as I went. She laughed at me and cursed the wealthier classes, but I took no notice and carried on scrubbing. Then suddenly the woman pushed me from behind with her foot.

I saw red. I grabbed the foot and pulled the woman to the ground. I got on top of her and beat her with all the strength I had. Immediately the other girls started to sing and shout as loud as they could and one of them stood at the door covering the peephole with her head. I could not stop: I wanted to kill the woman in my rage. I beat her and scratched her; I tore at her hair. And every time I hit her I felt better. Every blow was relief from the months of tension, fear and suffering. I used my hands, my feet and my teeth until I could do no more. From sheer exhaustion I stopped and stood up. The woman was a shocking sight and could not move. I stood panting as she was dragged to a corner. In my stomach I had terrible pains and I was near to collapse as the woman silently watched me when I fell to my knees again and finished scrubbing the floor. For the rest of the day I felt ill and a great depression came on me when I thought of my baby.

Nina and her friends were delighted by my fight. It made the gang stronger still and I acquired as much respect as any of them. Even the woman I had beaten eventually became friendly; she said 'good morning' to me a few days later and afterwards came over to talk to me often.

Some of the men prisoners, I noticed when the door was open, worked in the passage outside. They scrubbed the floors and whitewashed the walls and often called out to us. Two days after the fight, one of the men pushed a small packet through the door when we were being given our food.

'It is for the girl with the long hair,' he whispered. 'The boys upstairs sent it.'

I flushed with embarrassment as I opened the packet, but the other girls were delighted. Inside were five cigarettes and I shared them around the gang. They were the first cigarettes we had seen for a long time and each of us had several puffs, blowing the smoke towards the windows so that the guard would not notice.

That night there were taps on the ceiling above. I could not understand what they meant but Luba did. She took the broom and tapped on the ceiling in reply to the men in the cell on the top floor, who were asking how many of us there were in our cell and where we came from. They asked our names and everyone laughed as one message came through: 'What is the name of the girl with the long hair?'

But my hair was worrying me now. It was already June and the weather was very hot. We were not allowed string, ribbon or anything with which I could tie it up, and it was getting uncomfortable as it hung loosely down my back. At first the girls would not hear of it when I said it must be cut off, but finally they agreed to help me. One morning we performed the operation with an old razor blade which was hidden behind the cabinet. My waist-length hair was cut until it reached only to an inch or so above my shoulders.

On my ninth day in the cell Luba complained of feeling ill when she awoke in the morning. She had stomach pains and her head hurt, she said, and she was usually so tough that we knew she needed a doctor. It was an hour before the doctor arrived. When he put his head around the door and saw it was Luba who had called him, he said roughly, 'There is nothing wrong with you,' and went away.

Luba was furious, but she knew what to do. She asked me to bend down beneath a window. Then she climbed on my back and stood on the shoulders of another girl. Now she could reach the window which looked out over a road beside the prison.

Then Luba began to scream – ear-piercing yells which must have travelled halfway across the town.

'Help, help,' she yelled. 'They are murdering me, they are starving me. People of Russia, help, they are killing your brothers and sisters here.'

In no time the guards were at the door.

'Why are you shouting?' they shouted at Luba. 'Get down at once.' Luba climbed down.

'I asked for the doctor and I will yell until he comes,' she said. The guards hurried away and Luba began to yell again. Within ten minutes the doctor was back, standing just inside the door and leaving it ajar behind him. He was short and fat, with an enormous paunch; his nose was red and he had a small black moustache. Behind him we saw there was no guard. He was just beginning to reprimand Luba when one of the girls acted.

With all her strength she pushed the door. It hit the doctor in the small of the back and at the same time Luba sprang at him. He fell to the ground and she jumped on him, beating and scratching him everywhere, and we did not need any prompting as we began singing at the tops of our voices. Luba tore the doctor's shirt and pulled his red nose. We roared with laughter as she shouted: 'All the money you are given to treat us you spend on vodka, that is why your nose is so red.'

She did not stop beating him and pulling his nose for a full five minutes, but by now the guards had missed him. Two of them rushed into the cell and pulled Luba away and the doctor got painfully to his feet. He was bruised and scratched everywhere. He looked a sorry sight as he was hurried away and Luba was pulled outside. In a second we heard her scream again: 'If you touch me I will yell every day at the window.' Eventually the guards gave it up and pushed her back into the cell untouched.

Luba had done the job well. Every day after that the doctor came to the cell when we had finished exercise. Regularly he asked if we were well and was always ready to help. But he had only two cures: aspirin and castor oil. When our mouths became sore through lack of vitamins we complained and the doctor arranged that more vegetables were put in the soup. He became quite popular, but he never came to the cell alone again; a guard always stood at the door ready for trouble.

CHAPTER XII

The Inquisitor

At noon on the tenth day a guard came to the door, called my name and led me down the stairs into the exercise yard. There stood a black car with no windows except a small one in the roof. For half an hour, often over bumpy roads, I tried to sit until we jolted to a stop, then I was let out facing a tall building. I had no time to look around before I was led up two flights of stairs into a large well-furnished office.

Behind the desk sat a dark man with a hooked nose. He was in uniform, but he wore a rubashka, the shirt-like national dress buttoned up to the side of the neck and embroidered there, down the side and at the cuffs. He asked my name and I told him. He went to a large trunk, fumbled through the papers inside and sat down again with an open file in front of him.

He did not shout. He appeared to be friendly. I certainly was not frightened when he began to talk, but I was amazed at what he told me. He did not ask me questions then; he did not have to. He told me that my father was in German-occupied Poland, that my father's two sisters were in Warsaw, that my father had relations in Czechoslovakia and that they had visited my father in Poland before the war.

He knew where he had lived at Zaborol, he knew how many acres we had, how many horses, cows and pigs, how many people father had working for him. Indeed, he seemed to know everything. At last he finished talking about the family, looked up at me and said:

'Now about you.' I felt my heart beating faster and he continued as his eyes narrowed and his voice was no longer friendly. 'You were going to your father with secret information for the Germans.' It was a vicious, rasping voice. 'You are a traitor to Russia, the country which has done so much for you.'

Perhaps I had expected the spy accusations, but when he talked of Russia I could feel my temper rising. I tried to hold it in check.

'I am not a spy,' I said evenly, 'but if Russia ever deserved a traitor it is me. You sent me to Siberia to starve. I had done nothing against your country, but you sent me to die.'

The man leaned over the desk. His face looked cruel.

'You are a spy,' he rasped again. 'You received letters from your father when you were in Siberia. We opened them and we know that he was communicating with you in code.'

I laughed at him. I could not help it, but he went on. For two hours he questioned me, the same questions over and over again, but put in different ways. Twenty times at least he ordered me to admit that I was a spy and twenty times I shouted back defiantly: 'I am not a spy.'

At last he gave up. The questioning stopped and the man was wet with perspiration as he said: 'All right, you can go now, but you will come back again.' I was shown into the car and driven back to the prison. Completely exhausted, I was pushed back into the cell.

At exercise next morning I heard from Gunia that she had been taken to the same man the previous afternoon and he had tried to make her tell of the people I had spoken to on the way from Siberia. He did not accuse her of spying but said she must know of the people I had met because she had been with me. Then he had tried to bribe Gunia. 'If you tell me who the other girl met we will let you go at once,' he had said. But Gunia had insisted on the true story of our escape. She had admitted nothing else.

I expected more questioning at midday, but it was eleven o'clock that night when the guard came for me and took me in the same car to the questioner. A small light shone dimly on his desk, but a large and powerful lamp shone straight into my eyes as I sat in the chair prepared for me. I blinked and it made me feel sleepy, but not for a moment was I allowed to doze. I was questioned until four in the morning: the same questions and the same answers. Relentlessly the man went on and on, but he could not break me. I was still insisting, 'I am not a spy,' when I was eventually led from the room.

For the next three nights I was given the same treatment. At eleven o'clock I was taken in the car to the dazzling light and the ruthless questioning, and never was I back in the cell before five in the morning. It was impossible to sleep during the day. I was getting weak and ill and on the fourth night I could stand it no longer. I fell fast asleep as the light glared almost into my brain.

It could only have been for a second and the man was shaking me roughly to keep me awake. 'Don't sleep,' I heard his voice in the distance say. 'There are more questions for you yet.' I woke with a start.

'Why do you ask me the same questions?' I shouted. 'You have all the answers written down. Why do you waste your time when you could sleep as I do?'

He was furious. 'When you first came here you were nice,' he screamed, 'but now you are like the others. You are like the girls of the underworld, rough, rude and belligerent.'

I screamed as loudly back: 'You have made me like this. When I came here I was a good girl. But you do not know decency, you have taught me to be rough and common like the rest.'

I was parched and asked for water, but the man refused it. Then suddenly he gave up, ordered me from the room and shouted vile threats after me as I was taken back to the car and my cell.

After the fourth night they did not call me again for many days. Then, once more at eleven o'clock, I was driven back through the darkness to the man with the hooked nose. The bright light was switched on again, but now the questions were all of Germany: which part of Germany was I going to; who were my friends in Germany; what were the names of the people who were spying for Germany?

Tonight, thank God, I was not tired and as quickly as the questions came I snapped back the answers. I was making for the place I was born, I told him. I hated his country and did not want to see it again. But I was not a spy for Germany. I knew no Germans. He could not shake me. He cursed and swore at me, but it made no difference. He gave up early. I did not see him again for some time.

Now it was Summer and almost impossible to sleep in the heat and stench of the cell. New arrivals came and they talked of nothing but war. Everywhere, they said, were huge concentrations of troops; the roads were lined with tanks and airfields were everywhere.

One morning, when we went down to wash, I was waiting for the other women and had time to climb to a window. I was there for only a few seconds before a guard pulled me down, but I had time to see the beautiful green fields of the countryside and the huge expanse of corn sweeping up the gentle slopes of the hills.

Back in the cell I told the other girls: 'If war is on its way it is coming soon. If the Russians retreat they burn the crops as they go. But now the corn is still green, the Germans need food; they will come for it before it is ripe and the Russians can burn it.'

I was taken for interrogation once more, but it was during the day and lasted for an hour. The man with the hooked nose and embroidered rubashka seemed half-hearted. I am sure he knew it was useless to try to make me admit to being a spy. He scarcely shouted at me; it seemed almost as though he was appealing to me, but I admitted nothing.

The following morning we were at exercise when on the ground I suddenly caught sight of something coloured. As I came to it I bent and picked it up: a tiny flower, something like a sweet pea, which must have blown over the high walls. It was wonderful to see, for inside the prison there was nothing but concrete and whitewash. My thoughts flew back to the lovely flowers at home, but they were shattered in seconds as suddenly a guard took me by the shoulder, demanding whatever it was I had picked up. I drew back and refused. After so long without seeing a blade of grass I would rather have been beaten than give up that flower. Quickly one of the women told the guard what I had found and he walked away. Perhaps he, too, was thinking of home.

I took the tiny flower back to the cell and everyone crowded round to see it, even the old women who seldom moved from their places against the walls. We looked at it for hours, the only ray of cheerfulness, however tiny, we had had in weeks.

It was because so many of the women stayed in the cell at exercise time that I always carried with me my few pieces of jewellery tied in a handkerchief. Never did I move without it and one morning when we went down to wash I put the handkerchief on the shelf above the basin. For some reason the guard was hurrying us more than usual that morning, and I was back in the cell before I realized that I had left the jewellery behind.

I was frantic. I banged on the door and asked the guard if I could go back to the washroom. I had left something there I told him. But he would not let me go. 'Tell me what it is and I will get it for you,' he said. I dared not tell him and asked to see the governor. The guard shut the door.

All that day I sat worrying about the jewellery, but the guard did not take me to the governor. Still he had done nothing and when next morning the bread ration came I refused to eat mine. Soon the guard found the ration left over and demanded who had not eaten. I asked again to see the governor, but nothing happened all that morning. At midday and in the evening I carried on my hunger strike, and the following morning, too, my bread was left. Still the guard would do nothing for me.

By lunch-time I was determined to do something more drastic and took my soup in the tin plate. But I did not eat it; I waited for the guard to come in for the empty bowl and then I threw it, plate as well, full in his face.

The guard screamed at me, grabbed me by the arm and dragged me outside. I kicked and fought and shouted that if he touched me I would scream at the window for days like Luba. At that he let go of me and asked why I had thrown the plate.

'For two days I have been asking to see the governor, but you have not taken me,' I yelled. 'If I do not see him I will starve myself to death, then there will be an inquiry and you will be in trouble.'

He put me back in the cell, but in half an hour I was led to the governor's office and asked why I had assaulted the guard. The governor looked stern as I explained that I had left something in the wash house. 'What was it?' he demanded and I replied, 'Jewellery.'

The governor waited a moment before he spoke again. It seemed as if he did not want to be hard. Then I heaved a sigh of relief.

'I know,' said the governor. 'I have it.'

But the jewellery was not returned to me. Instead I was given a receipt and told that I should have given it up when I entered the prison. It was the last I saw of the pieces of jewellery I had treasured so much, but I still had mother's ring, sewn behind a button. And I still had my silver Madonna.

The days had become hotter and conditions in the cell were almost unbearable. The smell from the bin under the cabinet was terrible and we had to find a way of getting fresh air. Nina thought of one. For days we threw our water into the bin and then complained that we had no water. Two girls were allowed out to get more and the door was left open. Then we complained that the bin was full and it had to be taken away and emptied. For ten minutes or so the door was left open, the cooler air from outside blew in and for a while we felt better.

Time dragged on and with each day we heard more rumours of war. On Sunday morning, June 22nd, we saw that the guard was wearing a gas mask slung at his side in a khaki-coloured tin and other equipment as though ready to march. We asked him why, but he made an excuse that there had been an exercise. Night came but the light over the door was not switched on.

When the guard came with our supper he carried a tiny candle. We asked him what was wrong with the light and he told us it had fused. In the darkness we sat eating our soup. Something strange was happening, we knew, but we were not sure what it was. The governor came that night as usual to call the roll, but still the lights did not go on. He held a candle over the list as he called our names, but he could not see to count as he had done hitherto.

It was very late that night when finally I fell asleep. From every corner of the cell came excited chattering. I could not have slept long before the noise of the door opening woke me. The guard's rough voice was calling: 'Eugenia Laessig,' and I answered. Through the darkness came the voice again: 'Come at once, you are for questioning.'

Hurriedly I felt around for my boots, but I could not find them in the blackness. The guard would give me no time; he was calling again. Barefooted I made my way round the sleeping bodies and followed the guard, expecting to be taken again to the car. But it was not there tonight; instead I was led across the yard to the admission block, and by the light of a small torch I was shown up the stairs and into an office. On the table were three candles and the windows were covered with blankets.

Behind the table sat my hook-nosed questioner in uniform; he was a high officer, I could see by the squares on his collar, and he was looking very officious.

From his very first words he was rude and angry. For a short while he went over the same old questions and then suddenly said: 'Why don't you admit you are a spy?' For the hundredth time I denied it, but by now he had completely lost his temper.

'Admit it, admit it!' his voice was hoarse. 'For the sake of peace for all of us, why don't you admit you are a spy.'

No more could he rouse my temper. I looked at him and calmly replied: 'If there is a murder in the town and you are asked to admit it, would you do so if you had not committed the murder?'

The officer was beside himself with rage. He banged on the table with his fist: 'We have ways of making people like you talk,' he screamed and from a drawer he pulled a long sheet of paper.

Round the table he walked and stood over me, pointing to the paper lying on the desk. 'We have a statement from your brother Jurek,' he said and my heart leapt. 'We have captured him and he has told us everything.' The officer waited until the effect of his words had sunk into my mind. 'Your brother has admitted that he is German and that he was trying to get to your father in German-occupied Poland,' he said.

Quickly I tried to work out if this was a trick. Even if it were not, I decided that it could make no difference to what I had already said.

'You are lying,' I said to the officer. 'I do not believe a word you have said. I do not know if you have my brother or what he has said, but he can say what he likes. I am not German and will never say that I am. I am not a spy for Germany.'

'Ah!' The Officer let out a cry of triumph. He picked up the paper in front of me and put it a few inches from my face. 'We have it here. We have the proof. Here is your brother's statement. Here is his signature!' I looked at the writing at the

bottom of the page; it could have been Jurek's signature. I
did not know, I could hardly see it. Again I looked at the
officer.

'Whatever you show will make no difference,' I told him
quietly. 'You will never make me admit to spying.'

For another hour he paced the room, shouting threats,
bending over me yelling. From the drawer he pulled another
sheet of paper, put it in front of me and screamed: 'Sign it, you
filthy spy.' I refused and he bent over me again; his teeth were
clenched tightly together and his eyes were almost closed.
'Sign it or we will kill you,' he shouted.

But I laughed in his face; he was so near that I wanted to spit
at him. 'I know you do kill people in Russia, but I don't think
you will kill me.' Even now I could not lose my temper.

It was too much for my inquisitor. He raised his hand and
instinctively I drew back and waited for the blow. But it never
came. At that moment a terrible noise came from somewhere
outside. I gripped the chair. It was like a terrifying whistle and
the tearing apart of metal all in one. The officer stood with his
hand still raised, like a statue – one, two, three, four seconds and
then the crash. The whole building shook as though it were going
to topple over.

From all around came the sound of crashing glass and the air
was filled with dust. Almost before the last reverberating sounds
of the explosion had died away there came a second whistling
through the air. One, two, three, four seconds and the building
rocked again. I heard the rumbling sound of falling masonry as
the ear-splitting noise of the second explosion died down. More
glass was crashing, the windows of the office had been blown out
and the blankets covering them had been sucked outwards and
flapped in the breeze.

I did not move from the chair but now, fascinated, I was
looking at the hook-nosed NKVD officer. Slowly he lowered his
hand and he was trembling, his face deathly pale. Quickly he
blew out the candles, and I could not see him, but I knew he was
somewhere near and could not resist asking: 'Aren't you afraid
now?'

From the darkness I heard his voice, but he was talking with
difficulty. 'What do you mean? What do you know about it?' I

laughed back at him, enjoying the situation. 'Don't be silly,' I called, 'what do you think were coming down, eggs? They were bombs.'

'How do you know?' I heard the voice again and I was still laughing, 'I heard them before when the war started,' I said. 'That is the way the Germans bomb.'

Stealthily he was moving around the room and I could hear his movements. 'Where are you?' he suddenly called out and now I was sure he was afraid of me, afraid that I was going to attack him. 'Where are you?' he called again, but I did not answer. I could hear his heavy breathing and knew he was trying to edge to the door. 'Don't move,' he shouted and his voice was sharp with panic. 'Don't move! Stay where you are!'

It was too much for me. I laughed out loud again and he must have thought I was about to pounce. He shouted with fear, but he had found the door. I heard him go through it and heard him screaming outside for someone to help him down the stairs.

For a full five minutes I sat there, expecting more bombs, but no more came. From outside now I could hear shouts and the sounds of people running. Then a voice shouted up the stairs: 'Is someone there?'

I called back in reply and a guard came into the room with a lighted match in his hand. From outside came a frenzied command: 'Put the light out, they are coming again.' The guard blew out the match, took me by the hand and led me through the passage and down the stairs.

Down below was the large reception room and the guard told me to go there and wait. But now the room was in a terrible state; the ceiling had crashed in and the floor was covered with broken plaster. I carefully picked my way through it. Next to the reception room was a large office and someone was there; I could hear every word he said as he shouted into a telephone. One bomb had exploded in the big exercise yard, the second had hit the sentry box in the corner of it, killing one of the guards. 'Yes,' I heard, 'he is dead. He was smoking a cigarette.'

The second bomb had blown out a wall in the male prisoners' block and many of them, I heard, had been injured by falling bricks and masonry. But none of them, and I thanked God as I listened, had been killed. All over the prison the windows were blown out and the wooden shutters blasted away. Everywhere the prisoners had panicked; many of them had rushed through the smashed doors and now the guards were trying to round them up.

I sat listening to a full report of the bombing until there were more footsteps and I heard a second voice say: 'There is someone in the reception room, it is a woman.'

Another voice came through the darkness: 'If she were there before the bombs fell she is dead; the ceiling came down.' Heavy footsteps followed and a voice at the door asked: 'Who is there?'

I shouted my name and a young guard came in, took my hand and led me out, asking which was my cell. The exercise yard was covered with broken glass, and I stopped. 'I cannot walk over that,' I told the guard, 'I have no shoes,' and he picked me up and carried me across the yard to the cell block. 'Don't be afraid,' he kept saying and as kindly as possible. I recognized him as one who had several times passed us cigarettes.

As he led me up the stairs he told me to keep to the wall to avoid the glass and we reached my cell. I could hear the panic among the women inside, and as the guard opened the door they rushed at it, trying to get out. He pushed me in quickly and slammed the door.

Nina rushed to me. 'We thought you were dead,' she said and the other women gathered around. 'What's happened?' they all asked at once, and I told them everything. No one tried to sleep again that night; the guards constantly patrolled outside, but there was noise everywhere, because everyone was afraid that more bombs would soon fall. We were not allowed out for exercise next day and at night not a light could be seen.

In the cell things at last became quieter, but on the following day we saw a young Russian girl hand a note to the guard. No one knew what she had written, but she appeared to be pleased with herself. The girl was a strict Communist and it eventually transpired that she had written to the governor, telling him that I had talked of what had happened and had said that I knew the Germans were coming.

'You see,' the Russian girl had whispered to others in the cell, 'she is a German spy; she knew exactly what was going to happen.'

Soon the governor was at the cell door and I was called into the corridor. 'You have been spreading the news,' he said, and I waited for his next words, feeling certain that I would be punished. But his voice was kind and tired.

'I am not your inquisitor. If you are a spy you could do harm outside, but in here you cannot,' he said. 'If you know what the Germans are going to do, don't spread rumours among the other prisoners. We must have no panic.'

He said no more, but turned away wearily as I was sent back into the cell. But Nina and the gang were not satisfied and even the growing darkness in the cell could not save the Russian girl now. They found her and beat her into unconsciousness. The following morning she asked to be moved and was taken away. She told the guard that she would be killed if she were left with us, which I believe would indeed have been her fate had she stayed another day, for she was a spy among us and we had no time for spies.

Soon the news reached us that Russia and Germany were at war. It had started on the previous Sunday, June 22nd, the day the first bombs fell and all around Proskurov, we heard, were tank concentrations and new airfields. With no declaration of war the Germans had attacked all along the border and the white prison had been mistaken for a military target.

With no shutters to the windows now we could see what was going on outside and took turns at being lifted to the windows to report the tanks and army lorries as they poured through the town. We had also a better means of communication with the men prisoners upstairs; we fixed messages to a spoon that was hauled up on a string from the window above. Every scrap of news was passed on; the men even sent down cigarettes.

On the third night the planes came again; through the window we could see the searchlights and the noise of the anti-aircraft guns all around was deafening. We fell flat on our faces as dozens of bombs crashed down. Luckily the prison was not hit but shrapnel fell like rain on the roofs and some went through a cell on the top floor. We were frightened and many of us prayed time and again; but now we prayed for the Germans to advance as far as Proskurov so that they could free us.

Night after night the planes came, but somehow we were not hit again, and day after day women were crammed into the cell, all accused of spying. One poor girl had been a companion to a Russian Commissar's wife; they had sheltered in a cellar from the bombing and she had been asked to go upstairs to find something. She told us that she had struck a match and had been arrested for sending signals to the German planes. Another woman we were sure was a spy; she was about forty, a well-dressed doctor. A radio transmitter had been found in her house and she seemed to be proud of everything she had been accused of. Never once did she openly admit that she was a spy, but she told us how nice the Germans were and how well we would be treated when they arrived.

But now we had a new worry. At exercise we began to see that many of the cells were empty and quiet; some of the men were already being evacuated and we feared that we might follow them.

New girls in the cell told us how the Germans had advanced with astonishing speed, that their line now stretched from Leningrad to the Black Sea, and that they had occupied Rumania. We heard that they bombed everything that moved and even machine-gunned people working in the fields, but we could only look on them as possible saviours.

Then one morning we realized our hopes were quickly fading. Usually we were taken for showers every Thursday, but now it was Tuesday and the guard was ordering us all to the shower house. We were hurried along at the double; seconds only were we allowed under the showers, then at the double again we were rushed back to the cell. We had no time to recover our breath when the next order came; it was to file out to have our fingerprints taken.

We thought of every possible way to delay the guards. Many of the girls objected to having their prints taken on religious grounds; they said that they would go to hell if they agreed, but the guards would not listen. We fought them, we cried, and time after time we slammed the cell door and had to be dragged out, but the guards won. By midday they had dealt with all of

M

us. Then our soup was brought in and we were told to hurry through the meal.

We were still eating when the key turned in the lock again and screams arose from every corner of the cell. But it was me alone they wanted. I was marched to a room near the reception hall and my hook-nosed questioner was awaiting me once more.

This time he was not alone. Several prison guards sat in the same room and hook-nose shifted uncomfortably in his chair.

'Here is your statement,' he said, and he spoke almost apologetically. 'Would you sign it?' He handed me ten sheets of close typing. My fingers quickly flicked them over and I almost laughed. I picked up the statement and handed it back to hook-nose.

'I will not sign it,' I said. 'It is in Russian and I cannot understand it. I may be signing my own death sentence.'

At once hook-nose knew that I was trying to defeat him again. He forgot the guards and his voice rose to a shriek. 'Sign it,' he yelled. 'You speak Russian. Why don't you understand it?'

I answered: 'Yes, I speak it but I do not read it. If you write it in Polish I may be able to help you.'

Now the prison guards were grinning. I am sure they hated the NKVD as much as I did. They dared not say a word, but I know it was only their presence which stopped hook-nose from striking me. Instead he paced the room in rage, mumbling oaths at every step until at last he stopped in front of me. He almost spat the words at me: 'You may go.' I hurried from the room before I burst into laughter.

At supper-time that night two guards came to the cell and one of them carried a sack. To each of us he gave an extra ration of half a loaf. 'Don't eat it now; you will need it,' he ordered and then told us to gather our belongings together as soon as we had finished our soup. From the road outside we could hear shouting and the noise of tanks and lorries. We cried, we screamed, but the guards took no notice. Nothing, it seemed, could save us now.

It was dark when the guard opened the door again and shouted, 'All of you, out.' It was no use crying any more. We filed silently into the yard below. We carried our bundles as best we could and an old lady of seventy leaned heavily on me as she staggered along to the jail entrance. Gunia hurried to catch up and walk beside me and I heard Nina's voice from near by. 'Pray God they don't take us to the railway station,' she was saying; 'if we go on a train the Germans will bomb us.'

Outside the jail we were lined up in the street, three hundred women and a thousand men. At every five yards stood an NKVD guard armed with a tommy-gun and holding an Alsatian dog on a lead. And against a wall I saw three grey-uniformed soldiers guarded by more soldiers with tommy-guns. They were Germans, the soldiers we had prayed would come to save us but now were prisoners like ourselves.

We moved off through the town in the darkness. Gunia, Nina, myself and the old lady were in the last row, and behind us came a truck which carried the belongings which had been taken from us when we entered the jail. Behind the truck marched three German prisoners.

Nina knew the roads well and for ten minutes her scared voice came out of the darkness as we went in the direction of the station. Then I heard Nina say softly, 'Thank God.'

We had passed the last road leading to the station and were heading out of town eastwards towards Vinnitsa. My boots were already hurting my ankles, for I had no socks now to protect them. Through the night we marched, shuffled and staggered for four hours, with the guards prodding at us with their guns, cursing and shouting at us to hurry. The old lady could hardly walk at all, and we half-carried her most of the way.

Somewhere along the main road we passed a long line of tanks, covered with a camouflage of leaves, and we learned they were retreating to Kiev to form a new line near the city. Then we heard shouts of anger; a tank officer was bellowing: 'Get these people off the roads, they must be kept free for the army.' Soon we left the road and stumbled over paths across the fields.

Some time after midnight on the morning of July 2nd we were halted. Beneath us the path was inches thick in dust churned up by the tanks, and from out of the blackness came the shout, 'We are stopping here, you can rest.' I sank into the dust where I stood; it was so soft and quite the most comfortable bed I had known for weeks. I was asleep in less than a minute, exhausted.

Gunia was shaking me, it was morning and the sun was blazing down. I had slept the night through and was covered with the black dust which the dew had stuck to me. I rubbed it out of my eyes and spat it out of my mouth. All around us were green fields, sloping away into gentle hills; fifty yards or so away was a stream and I quickly forgot the dust as I gazed at the beautiful countryside.

Not everyone had been allowed to sleep as I had; I saw there were now no more than a dozen of our guards left and the German prisoners had gone too. Orders were being shouted and the last of the thousand men were on the move; they passed us in long lines and marched out of sight.

From near by I heard a sudden shout; a woman prisoner and her young daughter were struggling with a guard. The woman's husband and son were in the line of prisoners and they were being pushed back into line with tommy-guns. Their anguished cries to each other were pitiful to hear, but soon the men's voices were far away and the woman and daughter were sobbing hysterically. Only God knew if they would ever meet again.

We were then ordered to form into lines of eight. Then the governor waited until we were quiet and we heard his voice again, in loud, clear words: 'Fall out the prisoners who are on political charges.'

I stiffened in terror. Why did he want us? I was accused as a spy and should have stepped forward. But I could not move, my limbs would not let me. In front of me was the woman doctor and I grabbed her arm. She appeared to be proud that she was being called. She was smiling and said, 'That's me.'

I held on to her arm petrified. 'Don't move,' I hissed. 'What do they want us for? It cannot be for anything good.' Seven women stepped forward and I held my breath as I saw that one of them was the young girl who had been accused of signalling to the Germans with matches.

Not a sound could be heard as three guards stepped forward and waved their tommy-guns in the direction of the stream. Not a word was spoken as the seven women obeyed the sign and walked down the slope to the bank. They stopped when they could go no farther, the guards had walked ten yards behind and they stopped too.

Nobody moved. For five seconds the stillness was agonizing, then suddenly the terrifying crackle of the tommy-guns blasted the quiet and stillness of the countryside. Seven women slumped to the ground, their bodies riddled with bullets; three of them fell into the stream and all was deathly quiet again. We watched as the guards turned and walked back to us. Not a soul moved, not a soul could find the voice to cry out. We stood like statues, every eye on the guards, waiting for the guns to be turned on us.

Twenty yards from us they stopped, their faces grim as they watched us like hawks; but the guns were not pointed our way. The prison governor slowly walked to a mound of earth, climbed it and faced us. My heart was thumping as we waited for his next words. I should have been lying with those seven women at the stream, and I was waiting for my name to be called but it never came.

The clear voice of the governor rang in my ears: 'Women, I have something to say to you.' His face looked sad and he was beckoning to us all with both arms. 'Gather around me,' he called. As in a dream I moved forward automatically with the other women; we had acted like sheep and we stood like sheep waiting for what was to come.

'Women, we can take you no farther. You are free to go where you please. I discharge you all.' Seconds passed, but still no one moved. Was this a dream, what were we hearing? Then in a flash the dream shattered and we realized that what we had heard was real. Suddenly I found myself turning with the rest of the sheep and I ran as fast as I could over the fields, with the governor's voice still ringing in my ears. 'Keep off the roads,' he was shouting, but I scarcely heard.

CHAPTER XIII

Flight through the Battlefield

In all directions over the countryside the women were spreading out, each one running as fast as she could. My feet were hurting, but it did not matter; I had no time to think of them. I was sobbing. I was laughing. It must have been a quarter of an hour before, from sheer exhaustion, we began to slow into a walk and now we formed into a small group of the mother and daughter, Nina, Gunia and a few others.

At the top of a hill we could see a main road, and columns of tanks and army lorries were pouring along it. Gunia wanted to make for the road but I knew that was dangerous, for the Germans would surely find those columns and bomb them. I could see a huge wood in the distance and that looked much safer. But Gunia would not agree; she argued that the Germans bombed woods and forests. So we split into two smaller groups: The mother and daughter and Nina joined me and we walked eastwards towards the wood.

Now the sky was quickly filling with ominous clouds and we were still not in the wood before the rain poured down. Within minutes we were soaked to the skin and Nina became frightened. 'Perhaps there are wolves in the woods,' she said.

'After all these months in prison are you scared of wolves?' I asked Nina and soon we were following a path through the trees.

We could not have walked for more than half an hour when we came to the far end of the wood and there, just a mile or so in front of us, we could see a small village. The rain still fell in torrents. We went no farther than the first house and banged on the door. It was a full minute before the door opened; an old woman stood there and a younger woman stood behind her, and from inside the house we could hear the chattering of children.

Both women were obviously scared. It was Nina who then took charge of the situation.

'We are from prison,' she almost shouted at the woman; 'we want food, at once, and a fire to dry our clothes.' The words acted as magic; the door was thrown open and immediately we were shown into the house. We might have been murderesses, anything, but the word 'prison' had its effect.

In no time the women lit a fire and we stripped off our clothes. From the garden they got onions and made a thick, delicious soup with milk; they gave us bread and watched us as we devoured the first decent meal we had in months.

Gradually we felt better, rested and warm, and the women lost their fear of us; our clothes were almost dry and we must have been at the house for two hours when Nina gave a shout from the window. Gunia was walking down the road from the wood with a group of other women; they were drenched and, like us, made for the first house they saw. We wanted to help them but to have them in the same house was impossible; how long we would have to stay we did not know and, with four of us already there, we asked Gunia to find another house.

Nina told her how to go about it. Demand food and shelter, she told Gunia, and if the villagers refused, then threaten them. We hated acting like this, but it was the only way and Gunia and the others soon found what they wanted.

As later the rain stopped and the sky cleared the planes came; whether they were German or Russian we knew not, but bombs thundered down through the night. Nothing hit the village, but we knew the war was not far away; at any moment we might become the next target and we decided to move the following day.

But now we had a difficulty: the woman doctor wanted to stay with us and she was openly admitting that she was a German spy. So far it had not mattered, but if we came to a village occupied by Russian troops this could be dangerous. We might all be shot as spies. Somehow we had to leave her behind.

The tiny village had filled up quickly with women from the prison; more than a hundred had moved into the houses, and soon, we knew, the food must run out. Nina decided not to join us; we had planned to make our way westwards and she wanted to get back to Proskurov. We said goodbye to her late in the afternoon and walked out of the village without saying a word to the doctor. Now our party consisted of Gunia, the mother and daughter, a girl named Helena, the two Polesian women and myself.

For three hours we walked, down into a valley, and made for a main road we had been told was at the top of the hill. The fields were full of ripening corn, the grass was green and the birds and bees were not disturbed by the distant rumbling of war. But my boots were hurting so much that I decided to carry them and walked barefooted.

The main road was full of troops and army transports, all Russian and retreating eastwards, and no one appeared to notice us as we pushed our way through the throng and made for the fields on the other side of the road. From the speed with which the troops were moving we felt the Germans could not be far away. So far we had seen no sign of them.

It was evening when we reached a village and still light, and we could see the beautiful trees around it, fruit trees with the fruit ripening, and flowers in the gardens in front of the thatched houses. The villagers ran into the streets when they saw us and asked us who we were; they told us that one of the women from our jail had already arrived and a woman went running off to find her. It seemed we were among friends until the former prisoner arrived, then my heart sank; she was the woman I had fought in the cell.

But she was more than friendly. She seemed genuinely pleased to see us; she told the village women that my father was a German general and that we must be well looked after in case the Germans arrived soon. In no time we were taken to a house and given the most enormous meal I had seen since I left Poland. Every woman in the village brought something, cream cheese, milk, white bread, pastries and meat. They made us drink vodka – to kill the germs we had brought from the prison, they said – and wanted us to stay in their houses overnight. But this meant separating and we refused politely until they took us to a large shed where we could all sleep on soft hay and straw. The noise of the guns and bombs could not keep me awake that night.

In the morning the villagers begged us to stay and brought us more food and milk. But we all had the same idea: to reach our homes as soon as possible. So we thanked them and started walking again. My feet now were blistered and I had nothing to cover them, and they were hurting at every step, but somehow I kept up with the others.

For hours we kept on until we came to another village. But what a difference from the friendly village we had left! Although we did not see them, the Germans had passed through. Many of the houses were burned and blackened and the villagers were unfriendly. They had no food; what the Russian troops had left the Germans had taken. They had even pulled up the green cotton shoots to feed their horses. All around us was the drumming of artillery. We passed hurriedly through the village. Our first contact with the war was frightening.

Now we were heading north. We had no maps but we knew that north was the general direction for most of us. Two of the women came from a village about twenty miles south of Rovno and Helena lived in a border town. We walked and walked, my feet torturing me, until we saw another village.

Just south of the village we came to a railway and were just about to cross it when we were stopped by a shout. A little way down the line were two men and they hurried towards us. 'Where are you from?' they demanded, and we told them Proskurov. 'Why have you left there?' came the next question and I replied that the Germans were in the town.

As we spoke I could see there was something different about the men; they did not have the broad faces of the Russians, but longish, good-looking features, and their hair was long and blond. They were dressed in grey, something like a uniform, though I could see no buttons.

Now I was afraid. 'Why do you question us?' I asked, but their answers were vague. 'Who are you?' I went on, and they told us they were Russian soldiers who had been ordered to Proskurov to join up with the army. 'Then why do you have long hair?' I demanded. 'Russian soldiers do not have any hair.' The men answered that they had been called up quickly and had not time to have their hair cut.

Everything they said made us more suspicious, they spoke good Russian but I was sure they were not Russians. We began to move off down the railway line and the men moved with us. 'May we come with you?' they asked but now we were scared.

'Stay away from us. We do not trust you,' I shouted and we ran into the fields. The two men did not follow, but we ran until we could run no farther. Then we sank into the long grass to rest.

Soon we were walking again, watching the sun to keep us in the northerly direction, and it was not long before we met a Russian. He was old and carried a huge bundle on his back and told us he was tramping from his own village, which the Germans had occupied. For a while he walked with us, then as he turned off he gave us a warning.

'Be careful,' he said. 'Hundreds of paratroops are dropping all over the countryside.' We were sure then that the men from whom we had run were German paratroopers.

It was evening again as, tired and hungry, we reached the next village. The houses were well kept and freshly painted; everything was neat and well laid out and the war had not yet come that way. Here must be food and shelter, and expectantly we went to one of the first houses. But no one answered our knock, so we went to another house. The same thing happened there and it was not until the fourth house that our knocks and calls were answered.

A woman opened the door and I could see at once that we were not welcome. No, she had no food, she said, and in seconds the door was slammed. Everywhere we went we got the same answer; everyone was unfriendly when we told them we were from Proskurov, and without Nina we could use no threats. I was nearly in tears as we walked to a grass verge beside the road and sank wearily down. We were famished and we could go no farther.

For nearly an hour we sat on the grass; dusk came and it seemed the verge would be our bed for the night. Then suddenly Gunia spoke; a door had opened and a man was walking towards us from a nearby house. He was tall and dark, his features were too fine to be Russian and when he spoke he was apologetic. The retreating Russians had taken all the food, he told us, but three of us could sleep in his house if we wished. Gunia thanked him but said we would rather stay together in such an unfriendly village and the tall man apologized again. He understood, he said, but he did not like seeing us sleep beside the road; perhaps we would like to sleep in a shed beside his house.

We did not need asking twice. Into the shed we went and made beds from the straw, chattering excitedly, and we almost forgot our hunger in our new-found comfort. Then, all at once, we stopped talking; the tall man was at the door of the shed; he had been listening but now was smiling. When he spoke I could hardly believe what I heard. 'A thousand apologies,' he said. 'I thought you were Russian, but now I find you are Polish. Please come into the house to eat.'

We looked at each other, no one spoke for a moment and Gunia was the first to move. Then we all rose and quickly followed the man into the house. Within minutes people were coming from other houses; food that had been hidden away from the Russian soldiers appeared as if by magic and in no time we were sitting down to a wonderful meal. We were among friends who could not do enough for us.

Now we knew the reason for the sudden change. Everyone in the village of Antonovka was Polish; they had settled down there many generations earlier and still lived according to Polish customs. Everything had been hidden from the Russians, they told us; even the young men were hidden so that the army would not take them for soldiers as they passed through. Our host produced his own son, a fine tall boy of eighteen who had been hidden for days in a hole dug in the ground and covered with sticks and grass.

The party was gay that night. Russian troops had passed by in their quick retreat and nobody expected them back. It was now just a question of waiting for the Germans, for the villagers preferred anyone to the Russian masters they had been under for so long.

I slept in a comfortable bed that night. Now that we were among friends we did not mind separating and the next morning I was given another wonderful meal. I wanted to stay; my feet were torn and sore but Gunia was impatient to move on. I agreed reluctantly but the villagers would not let us go until they had packed food for us for the rest of the day.

A small crowd of them stood in the narrow main street and wished us luck as we set off. All was quiet and Gunia talked excitedly of the distance we should cover in the day, but within minutes the chatter had changed to cries of fear. Three German planes swept low over us and we threw ourselves into the ditch as bullets sprayed all around. For minutes we stayed flat on our faces, shaking and too scared to move until the sound of the planes disappeared and a woman's cries made us look up.

Down the road towards us she ran covered with blood. She stopped when she saw us and we could see she was shot through the hand. We tore pieces of cloth from our blouses and dresses to bandage the wound as the woman, between moans, told us what happened. Just along the road, she said, the Russians had left a dump of ammunition and some sacks of rice. With other villagers she had been at the dump to get some of the rice when the planes swooped out of the quiet sky. Several villagers were lying dead at the dump; others were wounded and she was the only one who had been able to get help.

We helped her back to the village, to the house of the tall, dark man, but we knew now that we could not go on. The air was filling with planes and everywhere around us there were signs that the battle was raging. Bombs crashed down and shells whined over the village in a terrible cacophony of ear-splitting noise.

Miraculously, the village was not hit, but all through the morning we waited as the fearful noise came nearer and nearer. Then from a house we saw about a dozen soldiers run down the street and run behind other houses to hide. At that moment we saw the Germans for the first time; some were on motor cycles, more were on foot, darting for cover from one house to the next. The village was taken, and we waited silently as the Germans went from house to house holding their guns at the ready, winkling out the hiding Russians.

Not a shot was fired. Every Russian surrendered meekly; they were too hungry to fight any more and we saw them begging for food. The Germans threw handfuls of small biscuits which they carried in pouches at their sides and stood by as the Russians fought for them amongst themselves.

Then another search began. Through every room of every house the Germans went looking for pictures of Stalin.

They found only one picture and that was in the village shop. They burned the shop to the ground; nothing else was touched.

As the shop burned a column of German troops marched through, smart, clean and erect in comparison with the Russians we had been seeing for days. But the tanks did not come our way, they were advancing along the main roads. The Germans we saw were comparatively small detachments sent in to mop up the villages.

As quickly as they had arrived the Germans were gone; not one stayed in the village and the villagers now felt certain they would not see another Russian soldier. Soon everyone was in the street shouting and cheering; we were out there rejoicing too, and it was then that I remembered the day the Russians came to our house at Zaborol and stole everything we had.

Most of the villagers, I knew, worked on a large farm near by; the cows, chickens and farming implements were still there, but who did they belong to now? I shouted to the people to take what they wanted, but at first they were afraid to go to the farm where they had worked so long under the Russians.

For a long time they talked and argued as I tried to persuade them, until at last one man's courage made him move. First one, then another, followed him. Eventually everyone was with him. They crowded up to the farm and took everything they could lay their hands on. Soon they were streaming back into the village shouting wildly, leading cows and carrying cackling chickens. Rice, too, was brought from the dump along the road, for there was going to be a celebration feast that night. Truly those villagers had never been happier.

In the tall man's house was to be the largest party and all of us helped to prepare the food. None of the other girls would kill the chickens, so I agreed to do it. I had been in Siberia too long to be squeamish about such things and I would never forget what hunger meant. I took a large knife and chopped off the chickens heads as they struggled. That night the soup they made with the rice tasted better to me than to anyone.

Early next morning Gunia was impatient to move again and now we felt it was safe. To the south and east we could hear the sounds of the guns but in the north all seemed to be quiet. For the second time we set out among waves and shouts and walked until late afternoon before we came to another village. But this one was practically deserted and there was no food to be had. We trudged on, hoping to reach shelter later in the evening. When darkness came we were still in open country and exhausted; my feet were now badly blistered and every step was agony.

All next day, and the following one too, we trudged north. Most of the villages were deserted; in the rest the few remaining people had no food to offer us. I was in a daze; my tortured feet dragged me on until, in the second afternoon, we came to a field of peas. Greedily I made a meal of them, anything to appease the ache of hunger. When we could eat no more we crammed our pockets and blouses with them.

I was now weakening and always felt sick; day by day my belly felt heavier as I staggered along and the pain in my feet was unendurable. When on the second night we reached a village I could go no farther; I was in tears as a woman found some onions and made a soup with clotted milk. And when we found beds in an empty house I cried with joy. But I could not sleep; for hours I lay almost in a coma as the pain from my feet shot through my whole body.

I still had not slept when Gunia was ready to start walking in the morning, and I felt it would be easier for me to crawl on my hands and knees than walk. I dragged far behind the others. They had to stop for me often. I knew that I was holding them back, but I could go no faster. By midday I had collapsed twice at the side of the road. I begged them to go on without me, but each time they waited. Helena and one of the other women were almost carrying me when we came to a railway, and there on the line stood a small, flat truck on wheels. With the sun still on our backs we saw that the line ran north. We put our bundles on the truck and I was lifted up beside them. The truck ran easily and the others took it in turns to push. We must have gone two or three miles like this when two Russians spotted us and climbed on to the line.

Both were officers, we discovered, although they were in civilian clothes, and they told us they were making north to Minsk, over three hundred miles away, where they were hoping to join a guerrilla army which was forming there. They walked with us for several miles and pushed the truck, but they left us suddenly and made off across the fields when we saw an army camp in the distance.

By late afternoon we could see a town, a few miles away in a valley, and we left the truck and walked the shortest way across the fields. I cannot remember the name of the town; it was somewhere near Konstantinov and we hoped to get food and perhaps stay overnight. Certainly we would not have gone near had we guessed what we were to see.

As we turned into the main street of the town we saw groups of men digging large holes and many of them were sobbing as they dug. Women were everywhere wailing and screaming, and German guards wearing white armbands stood near with their tommy-guns trained on the men as they dug. For a moment we stopped near one of the groups and spoke to an old woman. She burst into a flood of tears; the town was Jewish, she whispered, and the men were digging their own graves before being shot by the Germans.

Horrified, we hurried from the scene, but only just in time. Less than a minute later we heard the rattle of the tommy-guns and I found myself shaking with terror as I tried to run. The screams slashed our souls, but we dared not look round. I forgot my blistered feet as I found new strength to escape.

We were still on the outskirts of the town when, rounding a corner, our flight was stopped by another and larger crowd. By the side of the road, on what appeared to be waste ground, was a mound, twenty feet high, covered with lime. Dozens of women were beside the mound as the crowd looked on and from all around us came shrieking and crying. Gunia inquired of a woman what it was all about, and then she cried out too; she begged us to run and we hurried past the scene. The Germans were taking few prisoners; only those who were needed for some sort of work were allowed to live.

For several miles we pressed on, the terrifying picture of what we had left filling my mind as I stumbled and tried to keep up with Gunia and the others. Soon the air was filled again with planes and the gunfire was so near that it was deafening. We did not know it at the time, but we were passing from one pincer of the German advance to another. The Germans were blasting one salient after another all along the front and then joining up the salients and cutting off the Russians left in the pockets. We met a long line of Russian soldiers going in the direction from which we had come, but we dared not warn them. We hid in a ditch as they passed; in an hour or so, we knew, they would be prisoners.

It was late when we reached the next village. None of us could go much farther and we decided to stay overnight whether the Germans were there or not. It was not long before we knew the situation for, turning a corner, we saw a hundred or more Russian prisoners in a churchyard. They cried out to us for food, but we had nothing to give them. Even if we had we would have hurried past, for Germans with tommy-guns were sitting on the churchyard walls, and we saw that they wore the same white armbands as those who had shot the Jews earlier in the day.

Farther into the village there were only a few German soldiers; several houses were still burning fiercely and we made for one that was well away from the fires. It was a long time before an old woman answered our knocks; she was shaken and full of fear, and she told us there was no food. But I gave her an old blouse from my small bundle of belongings and eventually she found some oats and made a rough type of bread. From another house we got a little milk and then Gunia and two of the women went off to find a house in which to pass the night, leaving Helena and the mother and daughter to sleep with me in the old woman's house.

None of us actually slept. A battle started near by and for hours bombs fell all around. The noise of the guns was deafening and we all lay on the floor, shaking with fear and murmuring prayers. The battle went on for hours and at dawn the noise was still terrifying. But now it was not the noise of battle, which had passed us by and left us unhurt; but a Russian underground ammunition dump near the village was alight and every few seconds the air was filled with exploding shells and bullets of every description as they went up in multi-coloured flashes like a macabre firework display.

It was later that morning before we dared try to move on, but we knew we could not stay. The battle was raging backwards and forwards and it was certain death to wait. I did not know how I could walk again, but how could I hold Gunia and the other women back?

Helena hurried to the house where they had slept, and within minutes was back. For Gunia had left some hours before. Helena put her arm around me as she broke the news. Was I hearing aright? After all we had been through together, had Gunia really left me? Helena pulled me closer as I burst into tears.

I did not see Gunia again. I never knew what happened to her, whether she reached her home or was killed on the way. But even now I sometimes pray that she reached her home safely and lived a happy life thereafter. Perhaps she is still in Poland. Perhaps one day we shall meet again.

Now we were four and later in the morning we set off, making a wide detour to avoid the blazing and exploding dump. The road and fields were littered with jagged pieces of metal and it seemed a miracle we were not hit before we were out of range.

Soon we came to the scene of the battle. Somehow and from somewhere the Russians must have counter-attacked, for everywhere lay the bodies of soldiers, Russian and German. Already they were beginning to smell in the heat of the sun and clouds of flies were everywhere. Dead horses and cows lay on their sides or with their feet sticking grotesquely straight upwards. Burned-out tanks lay in the ditches, and the debris and rubble of war littered the countryside for miles. To the four of us this was a new scene, and in curiosity we lifted the lid of one of the tanks as we passed. But we drew back in horror of what we saw; a soldier inside had been burned alive, and his body had so shrivelled that for the moment he seemed no bigger than a child.

Dozens of maps lay in the fields; we needed one and we rummaged among them until we found it. Then, just as quickly, we threw it away; we did not know which army we might be meeting next and to be found with maps by either side might have meant our arrest as spies.

N

For days we wandered the countryside trying to keep in a northerly direction. Many times during these rainy days we had had no idea where we were heading, for there was no sun to guide us. Once we found we had tramped eastwards through the rain for hours; then we spent more hours getting back on course. We passed villages that were blackened, destroyed and deserted by war, villages occupied by Russian troops and villages occupied by Germans. We sometimes walked without seeing a soul, but all the time we heard the crashing of the guns, and at the end of the day we would find a village, only to arrive as a battle started. At nights we scarcely slept as the struggle went on less than a mile away.

My feet were now in a shocking state; the blisters had burst and more blisters had formed on the skin beneath the wound, only to burst again as they were chafed and cut by the rough and jagged earth. I did not know where we walked or why; it did not matter, I was no longer human. The pain from my feet was not local; my whole body was afire as I stumbled for no more than a mile at a time before collapsing, to wait at least another hour before I could continue.

At times I was hysterical and called upon God to let me die. Once I passed out and Helena and the other women brought me back. They should have left me, but they refused. They were weak themselves but could not hurry for fear I would die if left alone. Theirs was a kindness that passed all understanding.

We had been travelling for many days in all when we came to the town of Konstantinov; in all this time we had scarcely made a hundred miles in the direction which was taking me home. And still there were another hundred and fifty miles to Rovno. At Konstantinov the Polish woman and her daughter branched westwards, but they would not leave me until Helena and I were safely in the care of Sonia, a girl who had been in our cell in the jail, but had been released a month before.

Sonia had little to offer; she lived in a small house with her mother, but somehow they found food and made me rest for two nights before I put my feet again to the ground. Even then I could hardly walk, for the pains were now in my bones. On the next day Sonia went to the German town commandant and

told him about me. She explained that I had been banished to
Siberia and begged his help to get me to my father in Germany.
Somehow, amid all the organization of a gigantic invasion,
Sonia impressed him; the commandant was sympathetic and
soon I was hobbling along to the headquarters with Helena, who
waited for me in the street.

Several officers questioned me, but at last they were satisfied
with my story. They told me to wait and in an hour I was taken
outside to where a German army lorry stood. It was going to
Shepetovka and I was told to ask farther help from the German
commandant there. The soldiers helped Helena and me on to
the back of the lorry and we waved goodbye to Sonia.

Shepetovka was fifty miles away and it was heaven to sit on the
lorry and watch the fields and villages pass by so quickly. The
Germans were helping me now and I felt sure I would not have
to walk those fields and roads again. I was happy and confident
when I was shown into an office at headquarters. But now there
was more organization among the Germans; they had been in
the town for some time and the officer I saw was of much higher
rank than the commandant who had helped me in Konstantinov. He questioned me, asked where I had come from, and
when I told him Proskurov he immediately sent for two more
officers.

The Russians were still in Proskurov, I gathered, and the
officers could not understand why I had not been kept there.
Then I remembered hook-nose. Were the Germans now suspect-
ing me of spying? They now asked where I had seen Russian
troops on my journey. My answers were vague. For some reason
I could not make myself help them and in the back of my mind
I thought of the few Russians who had helped me. I was a spy
for no one and I could see no reason why I should give information about the Russians.

I could see that the German officers were getting annoyed at
my failure to give them information. Then one of them saw my
bare feet, and he lifted a foot to look at it. The sole and heel were
raw and almost fleshless, and at that they stopped questioning
me; they seemed at last to believe my story. But at the same time
they refused to help me.

'We are too busy with the army to bother with civilians,' I

was told. 'As you have come so far you can get farther. Go now, you are wasting our time.'

I hobbled into the street to find Helena talking to two young men beside a small horse-drawn wagon. She called me over. They were Polish, she said, and were making their way back to Ternopol, a hundred miles south of Rovno. They were taking the main road towards Slavuta, said Helena, and had offered to take us too. I did not need a second invitation; they helped me on to the wagon and we jogged our way out of the town.

The road was quiet and we were soon exchanging stories. One of the men was wounded in the shoulder and they told us that they had been in a Russian prison when the German advance came. Nearly a hundred men were in their large cell when the Russians, before retreating, pushed machine guns through the spy holes in the door and walls. At first the Russians shot at the men sitting on the floor and many leapt aside to avoid the bullets. Then the Russian guards raised the guns and shot at the men standing. One of our two friends slipped and fell; others, who were shot, fell on top of him and he lay listening to the shooting until not a person in his cell moved.

For a whole day he lay there soaked by the blood from the men above him, afraid to move in case the guards came back. The next day, people from the town came to the jail and opened the cell; the guards and soldiers had gone, the Germans had arrived. He and his friend were the only ones in the cell to survive. I saw the bullet holes in their jackets, but they told me they had belonged to men who had been shot. Their own clothes were covered with blood and too bad to wear. They had taken clothes from their dead fellow prisoners. The wagon we were in had belonged to a Russian, but the Germans had given it to the ex-prisoners when they heard their story. They had been given a little food, too, and we thanked them as they insisted on sharing it with us. The day was wonderful, peaceful. The sun was hot and I was relaxed. We relapsed into talks about our homes and of happier times; the war could have been a century away. But not for long; columns of German tanks soon forced us off the roads as they headed south into the advance. Our progress became slower and slower.

Then suddenly out of the quiet sky zoomed a dozen Russian planes and bombs were dropping around us. We jumped into a ditch and for five minutes I lay on top of German soldiers who had got there first. All was then quiet; the planes had unloaded their deadly cargoes and we were back in the wagon again for five minutes.

Six times the planes attacked and six times we flung ourselves into ditches. Miraculously we were still alive when the last wave left and we were able to jog on our way. And now I was recognizing the road; Gunia and I had been arrested on it weeks before; we were near Slavuta.

It was evening before the Russian planes came again and forced us into the side roads, and darkness was falling as we came to the first houses. We could go no farther that night and Helena and I found a house in which to sleep; the two men were shown a shed in the garden. But there was no food to be had in the town. We went to sleep hungry.

In the early hours of the morning war came to us again. From above we heard the sound of planes, followed by the crashing of bombs. And from all around dozens of anti-aircraft guns replied. Twice the town was hit and the house in which we crouched on the floor was rocked until I felt sure that it would topple over. Fires started on every side. Then morning came, the noise stopped and we were unharmed.

In the afternoon we drove into the centre of Slavuta. We passed the police station where Gunia and I had been taken when we were arrested and I wondered about the two policemen who had given us cigarettes. Germans with bayonets guarded the building now. We passed the NKVD headquarters where I had been questioned, but it looked so different now. Gone were the yellowish-khaki uniforms; only grey uniforms were to be seen. For the police I could feel nothing but pity, but for the NKVD? Perhaps they were now all dead.

Helena's home was in the western part of Slavuta. With shouts of good luck we left the two men and their wagon to walk down a side street to Helena's house. Then I stood back, almost weeping, as I saw the reunion between Helena's frail old mother and daughter she had not seen for so long. We all wept as we went into the house. They insisted that I should stay until my feet were better; but I rested for only two days. There was hardly a thing to eat in the town and now I was so near home. I was still hungry when Helena walked with me to the road which led to the small border town of Oszenin-Krzewin. She cried as we went, begging me to stay longer. But the Polish frontier was only a few miles away. I had to get there.

CHAPTER XIV

Over the Polish Frontier

To reach Oszenin-Krzewin should have taken me no more than
two to three hours, but actually it took five. Within a mile of
leaving Helena the pain from my feet was again unbearable and
I staggered until I fell by the roadside to rest. I made another
short distance and then fell again. German transports passed me
every few seconds and many of them were going in the direction
of the border, but not one stopped to offer me a lift. I was
completely alone in the world. If I had not been so near to my
goal I could easily have stayed in the fields to die. I forced
myself on, sick, tired and hungry; I had no time even to die. And
then I saw the border town. In another mile I would be back in
Poland. I staggered along the road trying to run; I laughed and
cried. I came to a church and leaned heavily against the walls
to rest.

I was sobbing as though my heart would break and I felt a
hand on my shoulder. A woman was speaking and in Polish I
heard: 'Come my child, you are ill.'

She took my hand, and like a child I went with her as she led
me across the street to her house and gave me milk. I drank it
greedily and she gave me more. Still I was not satisfied; I
needed more and the woman gave. Then I rested for an hour
and felt better.

The woman wanted me to stay, but I had to go on. 'You are
one of our children,' she told me time and again. 'Stay here and
I will nurse you back to health.'

God knows how much I needed her care, but I was nearly
home and I started walking again. Down the main street I went,
but I had gone only a little way when I had to rest. I was
panting for breath and my head was swimming. As though in a
haze I saw two men walking towards me, their clothes ragged

and dirty. I saw a German soldier cycling towards them and vaguely my eyes focused as I saw him greet the men.

I could not understand, but quickly everything cleared; the two men raised their hats in turn and showed their close-cropped heads. Then from the German came the cry, 'You are Russians,' and he grabbed the younger of the two men and dragged him away.

I rose to my feet as the older man, about forty-five, ran to me; he was trembling and crying and hung to my arm. He was moaning; he would not let me go. 'I am Polish,' he said, 'but everywhere I go I am taken for a Russian. Help me, help me.'

How could I help? The man was jabbering like a lunatic; he told me he had been in jail near Kiev and had walked all the way from there, avoiding the Germans because of his close-cropped hair. Suddenly he pulled me along the street. 'Walk with me and I can say you are my wife,' he pleaded. 'Please do it to help me. My home is only a few miles away.'

I was too weak to argue. Out of the village we went and immediately took to the fields away from the roads that were choked with German troops, lorries and tanks. The man supported me as I staggered along with him over a hill. I was helping him, but he was helping me too. I could not have gone so far or so fast if he had not half carried me.

The noise of battle came only as a rumbling of thunder as we reached the brow of the hill, but now ominous black clouds gathered above us and in minutes the rain came down in sheets. Lightning flashed and real thunder filled the air. The rain blinded me and I stumbled at every step. I called to the man to stop, but he held my arm tighter and dragged me on. 'Please hurry,' he pleaded a dozen times. 'If we stop I shall be arrested as a Russian. Please hurry. I am so near my home.'

Down into the valley we slid and lurched. My eyes closed tightly against the searing rain. Every few steps I heard the man panting: 'Come on, quicker, come on!' and for another half-hour we went until the rain stopped as suddenly as it had begun. At last I opened my eyes and there before us in the valley I saw the tiny Polish village of Mohylany.

The man was hysterical. 'I'm home, I'm home,' was all he

could cry as he thrust me along faster and faster. We came to the
first houses and I saw people running from their homes. They
called to the man and cheered, but he did not stop for a second.
His eyes were fixed straight ahead and he could not have heard
the cheers. He could only mumble, 'I'm home.'

Around the bend in the village street he rushed me and there,
outside a house, I saw a woman holding a baby. In that second
the man let go of my arm and ran crazily the last few yards. It
was his wife with the baby he had never seen. I could not go
another step. Villagers were crowding around as I leaned on a
fence. I hardly noticed them, for the world around me was
turning in a stupid roundabout.

Arms were around my neck. It was the man's wife and she
kissed me all over my face. 'You are the angel. A gypsy told me
a woman with black hair would bring my husband back to me.'
I could hear the words, but they were a mile away. The crowd
looked at me as though I were a miracle. My hair was drenched
by the rain and looked black as it clung to my face. Then I
collapsed and sank into a beautiful, soothing unconsciousness.

I was on a couch inside the man's cottage when I awoke. A
woman was bending over me, pouring vodka down my throat.
Then she forced warm soup between my lips and gradually I
felt better. The cottage was now filling with people, for the
homecoming had started a grand celebration. Eggs, bacon,
butter and bread appeared as if by magic. It was wonderful to
see, but I could not eat it. My stomach was not used to the fat
and I was sick after a few mouthfuls.

It was not long before an old man came to me and asked
where I was from. His face was kind and he sat beside me as I
told him that I came from Zaborol and that my father's name
was Laessig. Then I saw his mouth open wide as he stared at
me.

'Laessig,' he repeated incredulously, and he repeated the
name several times. 'Your grandfather Laessig owned the land
all around this village. He bought it from the Russian government after the first war and sold it to the Polish farmers.'

He shouted for silence and told all the people in the cottage.
Someone remembered that there was a woman in the village
who had come from Zaborol and a man hurried off to find her.

Then the people stood silently watching as the woman looked down at where I lay. Not a soul moved as she said: 'Laessig, yes. I know the family, but I don't know you.'

For several minutes the woman stood shaking her head and no one spoke. She mentioned the names of my two aunts, Maria and Wilma, whom she knew as children, and then she remembered my father's name. Weakly I nodded and the woman's arms were around me. 'Yes!' she cried. 'You are Eugenia, you were a tiny baby when I last saw you.'

From around the room I heard murmurs of relief, but nothing mattered. I was falling into unconsciousness again as the woman's proud voice went on. 'My father was coachman to Eugenia's grandfather.' Then I was carried to her house and my aching body sank into a feather bed.

For nearly a week the woman would not let me move. Gradually she restored my appetite until I was eating strawberries and cream, cheese, rich milk and meat pasties. Every half-hour she massaged my feet with vodka until the flesh healed again and the skin became hard. She promised to take me to Zaborol when I was well and I did not argue. I was too ill to move at first and now I was so heavy with child that the woman was sure I would lose it unless I stayed in her care.

With every day that my health improved I became impatient to move on, but the woman was not going to Zaborol for at least another week and I told her I could not wait. At first she pleaded with me to rest longer, but as she realized that my mind was made up she did everything she could to help me on my way. From a neighbour she begged a white flowered skirt and gave me some of her own clothes so that I could look more presentable when I got home. I threw away my head-scarves and arranged my hair in a comfortable, upswept style. Other villagers provided me with shoes and socks and early one morning I set out on the last part of the long journey. Now my silver Madonna was in a pocket next to my heart; the boot in which she had been hidden was left behind with the rest of my rags.

There was little more than twenty miles to go. My feet were comfortable and I felt happy as I passed the cherry trees and the green fields and called to the birds. The village was nearly an hour behind me when a passing woman called: 'Aren't you going back east?'

I stopped, wondering why she asked such a question, and the woman came across to me. Then all the happiness left me. 'All Jewish people are going east away from the Germans,' she said. Without head-scarves she had mistaken me for a Jewess.

I told her I was Polish, but she shook her head. 'You speak like a Pole,' she said, 'but you look Jewish with your head uncovered.' She walked on. 'Soon you will be caught,' she murmured as she left. 'Soon you will be caught.'

I was in a panic. This was something I had not dreamed of. I remembered that all women in this part of Polish Ukraine wore head-scarves unless they were Jewish and I had nothing with me to cover my head. I could only walk on and pray that I would get through safely.

As soon as I came to the next village I knew that what the woman had told me was true. Everyone who saw me stopped and stared; some called after me, but luckily I saw no Germans and I hurried on again to the open road.

By midday my feet were swelling and hurting and I had to rest. Even after my long rest I was still far from fit, but I knew I had to make the journey before dusk and curfew. I sat beside the road for only a few minutes. If I was to make it in time I had to start walking again. Soon I was passing fields of barley which were being harvested. Dozens of people were working there and I tried to hurry past. But I had been noticed. The shouts swelled into a chorus: 'Look, the Jews are coming back again,' they called. There were laughs and catcalls.

'The Germans know how to deal with them,' they shouted and then someone threw a stone. It missed me, but now I was scared. I tried to run, but my feet would not let me. I hurried as fast as I could, but I was near to collapse. I had still not passed the fields and the catcalls were getting worse when a car drew up behind me and I heard a shout.

I stopped dead, for the shout was German. Two officers were sitting in the car and they called me to them as the shouts from the fields got louder.

'Are you Jewish?' demanded one of the officers. I was now in tears; I sobbed that I was Polish and told them where I had come from; from the bundle on my back I showed them the receipts for my jewellery I had been given at the jail. At last it seemed that the officers believed me. They asked where I was going and I told them Rovno. They spoke together in German and then asked if I understood Russian. I nodded and they spoke again to each other. Then one of them opened the door of the car. 'Get in,' he said. 'We have only a Russian map. You can show us the road to Rovno.'

The catcalls faded as we drove away. I was relieved, but I had no idea what would happen to me. Perhaps the officers planned to shoot me when I had finished helping them. But gradually, as we passed villages that I began to recognize, they became friendly. I told them my father was in German-occupied Poland and one of the officers offered me biscuits.

As we came to the River Horyn I saw that the bridges were destroyed, but every time we were held up I was able to take the officers on side roads until we eventually came to the outskirts of Rovno. They were grateful when they stopped the car to let me out. They even waved as they drove away.

Alone again I looked around me. I was in the Ulica Hallera and just down the road was the Red Cross hospital where I was born. For fully a minute I did not move. It did not seem possible that at last my journey was coming to its end. Slowly I walked towards the main street, crying tears of joy at every step.

I turned into the main street and stopped dead. A terrible sight stretched out before me, every house, every shop and the cinema had been burned to the ground. On one of the ruined walls I could just read a blackened plate; when I was last there the main street had been called Ulica 3 Maja, but now it had a new name, Ulica Stalina. A little way up the street was the corner house where our dentist friend had lived; now it was a heap of rubble, and when I asked a passer-by what had happened to the dentist and his wife, I got one quick word in reply: 'Russia.'

Everywhere I looked it was the same; ruins and more ruins. The population of Rovno had been three hundred thousand, but hardly a soul now walked the streets of desolation. Never again would I see the Rovno I had known as a child.

I made my way through the debris towards the suburb of Grabnik. Relations of my stepmother had lived there and they were the only people I could think of to go to. In the distance I could see the jail at the top of the hill, which was on my way to Grabnik. As I drew near to the jail I saw a crowd outside the gates where I had stood for so many hours waiting to catch a glimpse of my father. Now a crowd of several hundred women barred my way. Inside, I was told, were thousands of war prisoners and only those who could prove they came from the area and had been conscripted into the Russian army were being released. And the crowd of mothers, wives and sweethearts were waiting day after day in case their men should walk through the gates.

I was told, too, of the horror that had been discovered in the jail after the Russians left. One huge room had been bricked up and when the walls were broken down the bodies of hundreds of prisoners had been found inside. I felt sick. I pushed my way through the crowd and away from the terrible stories. I could stand no more. I passed a group of women wearing white armbands decorated with six-pointed stars; they were Jewish and they were crying, they had little hope of ever seeing their men again.

In twenty minutes I reached the quiet streets of Grabnik. Scarcely a soul stirred and I felt sure I would not find my stepmother's relations. Then, as I rounded a corner, I noticed a man coming towards me. I stared at him; my stepmother's brother Michal had been young and dark haired when I last saw him, but this man was old and grey-haired, though the likeness was so great that my eyes would not leave him.

Now the man drew nearer. He was level with me when I heard him say softly, 'Trycia,' the nickname I had had in the family ever since Jurek had tried as a little boy to say the word for sister, *sistricia*.

The man seemed afraid of what he had said, and he was hurrying on as I turned and shouted: 'Michal, it is you.'

Michal walked back towards me looking at me as though I were a ghost. 'Trycia, where have you come from? Where are the others?' he gasped.

Soon I was in his house with his wife and daughter. They had heard from my stepmother that I was in jail; the letter I had written at the police station the day I was arrested had reached her. No one had expected ever to see me again.

Michal told me there was little to eat; all they could do was to wait for my father to return and help them. Then Michal hurried off to the house of another sister and between them they found enough food for a small meal. We talked until the early hours of the morning, but even then I could not sleep. I was home now, among my own people, though a thousand depressing thoughts rushed through my head.

The news spread quickly that I had arrived and on the following day some of the villagers came from Zaborol to see me. Helka, the woman who had been my nanny, was one of them and, after tears of joy at seeing me again, Helka told me how workers on the estate had stolen everything they could find after we had gone to Siberia. Even the religious pictures we had left in the small house had gone, every farming implement which the Russians had not taken had been stolen by our people, our own tenants and workers.

I did not have time to get to Zaborol that day. Friends and neighbours, many of whom I had never seen before, called to see me and the house was full until the evening. Almost every visitor brought a gift of food – eggs, cheese, honey and meat – which was piled up in Michal's house. He begged me to stay and take over the estate, but I told him this was out of the question. I would stay a short while, I said, but then I had to find my father. Perhaps father would come back some day to claim the estate, but the decision was his alone. I could do nothing at the moment.

On the second day I went to Zaborol, walking alone along the lanes I knew so well. Now the countryside around them looked different. The fields did not ramble over the gentle hills as they had when I last saw them; they were divided now into smaller squares, and every type of crop grew on what used to be one huge field of wheat or oats. It looked now like the Russian farms I knew so well; the Russian plan of maximum production had been tried here, but I learned later that it had failed dismally.

Through the village I passed, and people stared open-mouthed at me as I went. I could see them whispering among themselves, but not one of them spoke to me. They were not sure of themselves. Siberia had turned me into a woman and my condition made me look much bigger. One elderly woman, whom I heard above the frightened whispers, said: 'It can be no one else. It is Eugenia, the master's daughter.'

But they shrank away from me. Perhaps they had been among those who had stolen from the estate, I thought. Or perhaps they were fearful that I was not real. They looked at me as though they thought I had come back from the dead.

Looking straight ahead I came to the edge of the estate and passed the lake. I had just taken the road which led to the big house when a horse wagon caught up with me and stopped. It was one of my father's workers. There were tears in his eyes as he greeted me; he asked where my father was and begged me to stay and take over the farm. I told him I was merely visiting before going to Warsaw to see my father and said I was going to the house.

The man's head dropped and he looked down: 'Don't go, Miss Eugenia,' he said quietly. 'It will make you unhappy.'

He said no more. I thought he was going to cry and I left him. I turned a bend in the road and looked up over the hill between the trees to where the house should have been; but no house stood there now, not a brick was left standing above the ground. Only the cellars and the foundations remained.

On the gravel drive in front of the open space I stopped; the beautiful trees which had surrounded the house were no more and all that remained were five tall poplar trees which must have been too big to hack down for burning.

Memories came flooding back into my mind; the stone faces on the walls and the stone angels above the door, the room with the pictures which had always frightened me, the evenings beside the fire listening to father as he read stories to us or played the piano. And the day mother waved goodbye as she left for hospital and the birth of her third child, never to return. I sank to the ground and sobbed. Not a soul was there to see me. I sobbed until I thought my heart would break.

I was still crying as I walked to the chapel in the woods. From a distance I saw that it was still standing, but the sight which met my eyes when I reached it made me cry out to God. The door was broken and hung on one hinge. Inside the chapel everything had gone, the pictures, the altar, even the statue of the Virgin Mary. The place was filthy. Refuse and rubbish lay everywhere; it had been used as a dump and the smell of desecration was disgusting. I picked my way down the few stairs to the vault; the coffins of my ancestors were still there, but they were piled on top of each other and one was under a mound of earth. I fell on my knees and prayed. I knew then that I should never have come back.

For how long I knelt there I do not know, but suddenly I heard a movement near the door. From my knees I rose and walked up the steps. An old woman, dressed completely in black stood there. She was from Zaborol; perhaps she had heard me cry out as she passed by.

She excused herself for entering the chapel. 'No one ever comes here,' she said. 'You must be one of the family.' She was looking at my tear-stained face and she took my hands. In a whisper I answered, 'I am the daughter,' and then I was sobbing again.

The old lady gently led me away from the chapel; she told me the Russians had opened the coffins to search for jewellery. They had emptied out the coffins and left them on the floor of the chapel. The villagers from Zaborol had put them back and closed the coffins after the Russians had finished their work.

We came to Zaborol and the old lady led me to the house where my father's coachman, Karol Hubner, lived. I forgot my tears as I answered dozens of questions, then Karol took me to the farm and the villagers followed in a stream behind us, pointing at me and chattering as we went. The farm was nothing but desolation; not a cow, a horse or a pig was left; the farm buildings were overgrown with weeds and every piece of machinery was gone. Karol implored me to start the farm again; many of the people would help me, he promised, but I told him I must get to father first.

With the villagers still trailing behind, we went to the small house we had moved into when the Russians first came and from which father had been arrested. I did not expect to see any furniture, for we had received the receipts for its sale when I was in Siberia, but not even a pane of glass was left in the windows and the doors and stairs had been hacked away. I left at once; I could never live there again. I had seen enough that day and hurried back to Rovno.

The following day I walked to Aleksandriya, but even as I reached the river I could see that there was more devastation. The two bridges leading into the town were broken and lying in the water, and I was rowed across in a small boat. Most of the town was in ruins and some of the people who knew me told what had happened.

When the Germans advanced the Russians had left the town as fast as they could, but that night, when the Germans did not arrive, a Jewish boy of about eighteen had gone ahead to the Russians and told them the town was still empty. The Russians returned during the night and blew up the bridges just before the Germans came. But the Germans found out what had happened. So they set fire to the town and shot everyone they saw in the streets. A butcher I had known had been shot dead as he walked from his shop and every Jew that could be found had been slaughtered. I was horrified; for me then the Nazis were just as bad as the Russians. I wanted to get away from the town as soon as possible, for the smell of death still hung over it.

Before I left I went to the priest's wife, with whom Jurek and I had lived. She flung her arms around me when she saw me and we both wept. She had been so good to me and it was as though her own daughter had returned. Her husband, son and daughter were still there, but they had not escaped the wrath of the Germans; half their house was burned to the ground and they were living in one of the two remaining rooms.

From there I went to the Catholic priest for a copy of my birth certificate. I had no other identification papers which were recognized by the Germans and the certificate was the only way I could prove I was not Jewish. Then I hurried back to Rovno. I was tired and sickened by all I had seen in the past few days. I was glad to get back to Michal's house, where the war had not come to leave its horrible trail.

o

CHAPTER XV

The End of the Journey and the Birth of Marguerite

Three weeks passed before I left Rovno; each day I was working out ways of getting to Warsaw. Once an Austrian soldier tried to help me. He was from Vienna, a huge fat man who often went to my stepmother's sister's house to play the piano. The Austrian took me to the commandant in the town and my birth certificate was stamped. The commandant would not give me the nationality, but the fact of having any German stamp would, I hoped, help me. In a day or two a train would be passing, taking wounded soldiers to Warsaw and the Austrian hoped to arrange for me to take it. But when it arrived at Rovno the train was full and the officer in charge would not allow me to board.

Eventually, after several attempts at getting help from the army, I realized I would have to get money and somehow buy a ticket to Warsaw. Here Karol the coachman came to my aid. The silver zloty was still legal money and somehow Karol begged and borrowed enough for the journey. An elderly Jewish woman friend of my mother helped me with clothes; her daughter had retreated with the Russians and had left many things behind. Now I had an almost new pair of shoes, real stockings and two pretty dresses. I felt like a small girl wearing her first party dress as I looked at myself in a mirror.

Finally, when all was ready, I went to a Sudeten Czech who was working with the Todt organization, the labour force which the Germans had conscripted. He was driving in a few days to southern Poland and promised to take me; from a town in the south I hoped to get a train to Warsaw.

Early on August 22nd we set off in a lorry. I was loaded with sweets and food. Dozens of friends turned out to wish me goodbye and by lunchtime we reached Lvov, over a hundred miles south-west of Rovno. The town was in ruins and on the main road leading westwards hundreds of Russian prisoners were working, repairing roads which had been torn up by tanks and battle. The Russians called out to us for food as we passed and we threw them pieces of bread. Then I watched as they fought in the dust for the scraps. I felt sick at the sight and was glad when we came to roads clear of the prisoners.

Sixty miles or so west of Lvov the driver stopped the lorry; we were soon coming to the old border between Russian-occupied and German-occupied Poland and, despite the fact that it was now all German, the border restrictions were still in force and I had to be hidden. Under sacks, rolls of wire and old tyres I lay in the back of the lorry as we passed through Przemysl and came to a bridge over the River San where the border control was stationed.

The border guards asked the driver for papers and I held my breath as I heard them ask what was on the lorry. Silently I prayed I would not be stopped now. But no search was made and we moved off again over the bridge. I was now in western Poland and breathed freely again.

In a side road on the other side of the bridge I quickly came out of my hiding place and the Sudeten Czech driver took me to a small station. He had been wonderful and I gave him some of my silver money before he left. It was dark now and he warned me to keep off the streets as there was a curfew.

Suddenly, as I walked into the station, fear gripped me and I felt a fugitive again. It was the fear I so often knew at stations in Russia. At least a dozen blue-uniformed police were standing in a group and I hurried onto the dark platform away from them, scared that they would demand my papers and discover I had crossed the border illegally. If I were put in jail now, no one would know where I was and my father would not be able to help me. He did not even know that I had escaped from Siberia and was making my way to him.

For three hours I waited in the shadows on the platform until I heard a train approaching. I went to the booking office, asked for a ticket to Warsaw and was given two with the instructions that I would have to change at Lublin. Nervously, I pushed the silver money across the tiny counter and the clerk looked at it and then at me; although the money was legal, most of it was being hoarded and little was in circulation. Although it was only seconds, it seemed an age before the clerk picked up the money and gave me change in the new paper money.

The train was waiting and I hurried into the nearest carriage. It was only half full and I spoke to no one during the four-hour journey to Lublin.

It was still early morning when we reached there, but already the station was packed with people. Hundreds lined the platform and it was almost impossible to move. Everyone seemed to be carrying sacks of flour, potatoes, and food for sale. And they were all waiting for the Warsaw train to sell the food on the black market there. German and Polish police moved in and out of the crowd and I made my way slowly to the end of the platform and sat on the ground among the crowd. I watched the police, but they did not come near; hour after hour passed and it was eleven o'clock before I heard the sound of a train.

In a body the crowd scrambled madly forward and I was carried with them. I tried to reach a carriage door as the people fought each other to get in. But I was too weak; each time I was pushed back, the doors were closing and I was almost alone on the platform. I was in despair, exhausted and feeling faint as I burst into tears.

From the train I vaguely heard the shout of a guard, but now I had given up hope completely. Then through my sobs I heard a woman's voice: 'Quickly, there is room here.' Three pairs of hands were pulling me into a carriage and the door shut with a bang behind me. The train was already moving.

The carriage was crowded to suffocation. On every side I was being crushed until I knew that soon I must faint. A greyness was already floating around me as I heard the woman's voice again; she was squeezing out of her seat and I sank into the vacant space. 'You are ill,' I heard her say, but now my eyes were closed, my head swirled.

The woman was bending over me when my eyes opened again. She asked if I felt better and I thanked her for the help she had given. She bent closer. 'What are you doing here?'

she asked. 'You are from eastern Poland. Your accent is so soft.' The tears flooded again as I told the woman my story and gently she put her hand on my shoulder. 'Don't worry,' she said. 'I will help you find your father. I am a teacher in Warsaw.'

We took it in turns to sit and stand for the rest of the journey, until eventually we pulled into the Praga station on the eastern side of the river at Warsaw. Now I needed the help of the woman teacher even more. I could not have survived the mad rush to the station exit if she had not stayed close, protecting me with her arms as we were swept along.

I had two addresses from father's letters and the teacher chose the one she knew first. On a tram she took me to the centre of the city, to Ulica Natolinska, and my heart beat madly with excitement as we walked along the street until we came to number twenty. Outside the house on a chair sat an old man and I ran the last few steps to ask if he knew the name Laessig. The old man nodded and I asked if father was there. Then just as slowly his head shook from side to side. 'He's gone,' was all he said.

Quickly I asked the old man if he knew a woman named Laessig and he nodded again. Was she in the house? I was becoming frantic, but again he shook his head: 'She's gone.'

The answer was short and uninterested, and my heart sank. I wanted to cry and the woman teacher put her arm around me as we walked away. 'Don't worry,' she said and her voice sounded so reassuring at that moment. 'You have the other address. We will find your father there.'

On another tram we crossed the city and after several inquiries found Ulica Szucha. My heart was thumping again as I hurried to the second large house. It must be number two, the figure from father's letter was so vivid in my memory. But no, the second house was numbered three. There was no two. Time and again we searched the street before we noticed the small gate between the first two houses leading into what looked like a park.

Almost afraid now, I pushed open the gate and walked along the gravel path. On either side were tall trees. Then suddenly they stopped, and in front of us towered a huge mansion. Four tall pillars supported the porchway and the teacher led me to the huge carved door. Still afraid, I pushed and it opened with a series of creaks. Marble lined the hall and before us an open door led into a huge dining-room with a huge carved table and forbidding portraits that surveyed us from the wall. I backed into the porchway. Father could not live in such a place. I turned to go, tears of disappointment flooding my eyes.

Then I saw the tiny plate on the wall near the door. In tiny letters I read Foksal. I had seen it on one of my father's letters long ago. Foksal had been the name of the street before it was changed to Szucha.

A man was coming towards us from the garden. Quickly I could have hugged him when at last he answered: 'I don't know Mr Laessig, but there is a Mrs Laessig living here.'

It was at that moment I heard a voice from one of the upstairs windows. My aunt Maria was calling to her sister and I clutched the teacher's arm as I heard her call: 'Wilma, is someone asking for you?'

I rushed into the house at once. Up the broad stairs I ran. A door opened and Aunt Wilma was there. A moment later Aunt Maria was beside her and I fell into their arms sobbing as they smothered me with kisses.

It was minutes before we stopped crying and I could ask for father. He did not live at the house, my aunts told me, but at Lodz, many miles west of Warsaw. Somehow father had heard that I was in Rovno and that very day was trying to get permission to go to eastern Poland to find me.

Now I had a dreadful thought; perhaps already father had left Warsaw to go east, perhaps I had missed him. I wanted to rush to the government offices at once to stop him, but my aunts would not hear of it. They were sure father would come to them before he left for Rovno; he would not leave without clothes or food. My aunts told me I must look my best for my father when he arrived. One of them prepared a bath and they fussed around me and helped me undress. The woman teacher, meanwhile, was saying that she must go and I left my aunts to kiss her and thank her for all she had done. Then I was in the bath. I could not believe my journey was over.

I was still in the bath when I heard footsteps on the stairs.

Aunt Wilma was at the door and I heard her calling, 'We have good news.'

In a second I heard father's voice; he was shouting: 'Eugenia! Is she here? Where is she?'

I wanted to sob, I wanted to scream. I leapt out of the bath and cried out: 'Papa, papa!' The door burst open and there was father. I was in his arms and we were both crying our hearts out. It was August 23rd.

In a few days father took me to Lodz and there I rested for weeks whilst he worked from morning till night to buy black market food to build me up for the birth of my baby.

Early in December I walked one morning into the German hospital. I told the doctor: 'I think my baby is about to be born,' but he laughed.

'You are no more than a baby yourself,' he said. 'Come back in three months.' Outside a matron caught me as I suddenly staggered, and my baby was born in the hospital an hour later.[1] I clutched the tiny silver Madonna in my hand all the time, praying that the baby would survive.

I did not see her until the following afternoon. Only then did the doctors decide that she should be accepted as an Aryan child. If they had imagined the slightest trace of Jewish looks or blood in her she would have been exterminated.

I called her Malgorzata, the Polish Marguerite, for as she lay for the first time in my arms that day I thought of the aria sung by Marguerite in the opera 'Faust'. Mother had often sung it to me as a child and I remembered the words: 'Let me look into your beautiful face.'

Marguerite grew into a fine healthy child. She was still tiny when we again became fugitives from the Russians. As they advanced towards Germany we fled before them into Czecho-Slovakia. Finally we were saved by American troops who took us from the Czech border into western Germany.

And the war was ended, but not my fight to feed Marguerite. Again it was all slaving and black market until we took the train for the Channel coast and England. Never have I heard again of Kazik, the father she never knew, or his family. My stepmother

[1] December 12th.

and her son eventually returned to Poland. Jasiek was conscripted into the Russian army and thus escaped a living death in Siberia. Now he is in Canada, but never again has he seen or heard of his wife and child. Brother Jurek must have died many years ago. I am sure that somehow he would have sent news or found us if he had lived. Perhaps he was sent back to Siberia to die when he was caught. Perhaps he died in a Russian jail.

GEORGE ALLEN & UNWIN LTD

Head office:
40 Museum Street, London, W.C.1
Telephone: 01-405 8577

Sales, Distribution and Accounts Departments
Park Lane, Hemel Hempstead, Herts.
Telephone: 0442 3244

Athens: 7 Stadiou Street, Athens 125
Auckland: P.O. Box 36013, Northcote, Auckland 9
Barbados: P.O. Box 222, Bridgetown
Beirut: Deeb Building, Jeanne d'Arc Street
Bombay: 103/5 Fort Street, Bombay 1
Calcutta: 285J Bepin Behari Ganguli Street, Calcutta 12
P.O. Box 2314 Joubert Park, Johannesburg, South Africa
Dacca: Alico Building, 18 Motijheel, Dacca 2
Delhi: B 1/18 Asaf Ali Road, New Delhi 1
Hong Kong: 105 Wing on Mansion, 26 Hankow Road, Kowloon
Ibadan: P.O. Box 62
Karachi: Karachi Chambers, McLeod Road
Lahore: 22 Faletis' Hotel, Egerton Road
Madras: 2/18 Mount Road, Madras 2
Manila: P.O. Box 157, Quezon City, D-502
Mexico: Liberia Britanica, S.A. Separos Rendor 125, Mexico 4DF
Nairobi: P.O. Box 30583
Rio de Janeiro: Caixa Postal 2537-Zc-00
Singapore: 36c Prinsep Street, Singapore 7
Sydney: N.S.W.: Bradbury House, 55 York Street
Tokyo: C.P.O. Box 1728, Tokyo 100-91
Toronto: 145 Adelaide West Street, Toronto 1

OF BOMBS AND MICE

A novel of war-time Warsaw

MINA TOMKIEWICZ

Written with complete absence of bitterness or self pity, this is a deeply moving story of Nata and her small son, Bobush, battling through life in Warsaw before the ghetto uprising. Alongside this superbly realistic picture of their struggle for self-preservation there emerges a sober account of life under the German occupation which becomes steadily more harrowing and brutal.

Mina Tomkiewicz was born into a Jewish family in Warsaw and received her Master's Degree in Law just before the Second World War. Most of her family perished in the ghetto, whilst she and her baby son were two of the tiny number of survivors of Belsen. She has written here a powerful documentary, staggering in its objectiveness: a social commentary of lasting value and a tribute to the memory of those who died.

ONE MAN IN HIS TIME

An Autobiography

ALICK WEST

This is a personal story of this revolutionary century. It begins in a Warwickshire village in the age of Queen Victoria; it closes in the world of Stalinism. It tells how a child came to consciousness in a family where the Bible and *The Pilgrim's Progress* were living books, and how that peace and certainty were destroyed by the First World War. When after four years internment in Germany, Alick West returned home, that once precious word 'God' had lost its meaning for him. He strove to break from family and religion and to discover, as he thought, himself. To the question 'Who am I?' he looked for an answer in Ibsen, Nietzsche and Freud, and he listened to what those who loved him told him about himself. Then he read Marx, and at the age of forty he joined the Communist Party.

Here he has told how he came to make that decision, and what membership of the Party has meant for him. Whatever one may think of the author's political standpoint, this presentation of communism as the personal experience of a sensitive and intelligent individual throws valuable light on the great question of our time.

' . . . an outstanding autobiography – absorbing, important and with the most individual of flavours.' *ROY FULLER, Professor of Poetry, University of Oxford.*

MY THREE REVOLUTIONS

M. PHILIPS PRICE

Mr Philips Price, who was for over twenty-six years a member of the House of Commons, and was earlier a foreign correspondent for the old *Manchester Guardian* and *Daily Herald,* can truly claim to have lived through three revolutions. He can therefore write of them at first hand. First he was in Russia when the 1917 revolution took place; here a complete social upheaval occurred in line with the history and tradition of the country. Later he was in Germany and saw the early phase of the revolution that swept away the Hohenzollern régime. Finally, as an active politician he watched at close quarters the changes, some slow and some swift, that transferred the Britain of the Empire into the Britain of the welfare state, a revolution that is by no means complete, for the economic problems that have resulted have still to be resolved.

On an autobiographical base, Mr Philips Price records the events of a long life often in close touch with world-shaking events and his observations of over eighty years of changing society.

'This book, in all three parts, is an absorbing addition to the history of our times.' *Sunday Telegraph.*

'The comments on the world changes which the author has seen are shrewd and well balanced, and his impressions of the famous are discerning.' *Guardian Journal.*

' . . . it is written with that astonishing clarity that belongs to his generation and leaves the rest of us ashamed . . . this is a book much to be commended.' *Times Educational Supplement.*

SARDAR PATEL

D. V. TAHMANKAR

Three men dominated the Indian political scene in the last phase of the struggle for Independence – Mahatma Gandhi, Pandit Nehru, and Sardar Patel. Although to some extent Patel lived in the shadow of his two great contemporaries, the role he played was vital; it was he who made politicians see the inevitability of a break with Pakistan, and it was he who consolidated the country by abolishing the 600 odd states, creating the India we know today.

This is the first full-length biography of Patel to be published in Britain. It is the story of a great man, who in his youth had no interest in politics and did not care for Gandhi, who became overnight a follower of Gandhi and a front-rank politician.

RODNEY

DAVID SPINNEY

David Spinney presents a biography of Rodney which will be the definitive work for decades. It is not only an impressive piece of scholarship and exhaustive research, but a most entertaining account of one of Britain's great sailors. There is a wealth of background providing a lively social history of the times which helps us to see Rodney in the light of contemporary opinion. Rodney joined the Navy in 1732 and only ten years later became a post-captain. He took part in Hawke's victory off Finisterre over the French fleet in 1747, and in 1749 was appointed Governor of Newfoundland. During the Seven Years War he distinguished himself as a junior flag officer. His crowning achievement was his victory off Dominica over the French fleet in 1782. The other side of his story is less impressive. He was undoubtedly vain, extravagant and at times overbearing. David Spinney sets it all out, and there emerges a portrait of a vigorous, heroic, fallible sea-officer who has been ill-served by previous writers.

YANOAMA

DENNIS RHODES

Helena Valero was the daughter of poor white peasants living in a very remote quarter of Brazil, on the Rio Dimití, when in 1939, at the age of eleven, she was carried off by some of the world's most primitive people. With these naked warriors, the Yanoáma, who normally avoid every contact with civilized men, she passed a precarious twenty-two years in the immense and still unexplored equatorial forests.

Having returned to her own people with her four Indian sons, whom she had rescued from massacre, she was overwhelmed by the indifference and egoism of white people and had reached the point of regretting the Green Hell from which she had fled. She then met Ettore Biocca, a professor from the University of Rome, at that time leading a scientific expedition to the upper Orinoco. She gave him this simple but exact account of her experience, which was tape-recorded. This tale is quite unique: a record from within of a warrior society into which no man or woman has ever before been able to penetrate.

IBSEN *A Portrait of the Artist*

HANS HEIBERG

Heiberg describes in this book Ibsen's difficult childhood and youth, his many years' desperate struggle against economic difficulties, his sight with new dramatic material and his gradual recognition all over the world. He describes the small provincial town where a century ago the writer lived and developed and shows him emerging as a great playwright after years of adversity and humiliation. And while his fame grows steadily and spreads throughout the world, and while he himself withdraws into a legendary sphinx-like figure, the reader never loses touch with Ibsen the man. Heiberg portrays him faithfully, his little weaknesses, his vulnerability and touchiness, his love of honours, his prim orderliness. And yet never for a moment is the man's greatness in doubt.

LONDON - GEORGE ALLEN & UNWIN LTD

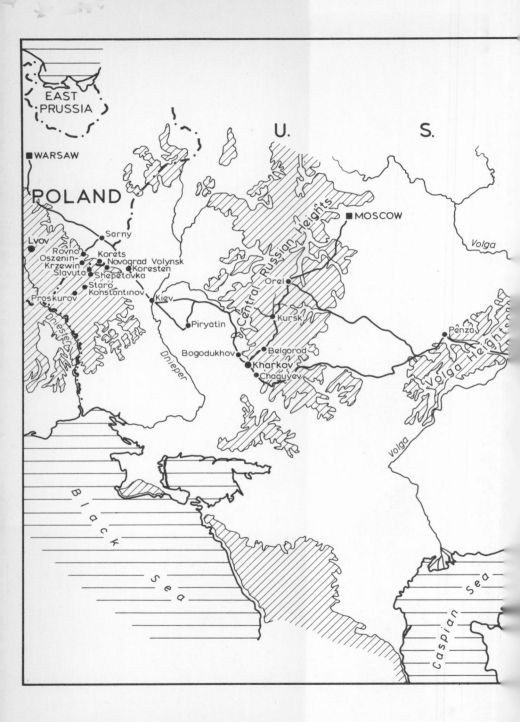